Perspectives on Terrorism
How 9/11 Changed U.S. Politics

Sponsoring Editor: Katherine Meisenheimer
Editorial Associate: Tonya Lobato
Senior Manufacturing Coordinator: Florence Cadran
Marketing Manager: Nicola Poser
Marketing Assistant: Laura McGinn

Printed in the U.S.A.

Library of Congress Control Number: 2002103939

ISBN: 0-618-25323-8

123456789-CRW-06 05 04 03 02

Perspectives on Terrorism
How 9/11 Changed U.S. Politics

Allan J. Cigler, Editor

Houghton Mifflin Company   Boston   New York

Contents

Topic Correlation Chart

The readings in this volume are designed to complement the coverage of most American government textbooks and readers. Many of the readings could be used in conjunction with a number of traditional American government topics depending upon the orientation and predilections of the instructor. In most cases, each reading has relevance to multiple topics. The following chart is designed to help instructors and students locate relevant readings that bear on nineteen typically covered subjects in the American government course, ranging (in alphabetical order) from bureaucracy to technology and politics.

Topic	Covered in
Bureaucracy	9,15,16,17,18
Civil Liberties and Rights	7,10,12
Congress and Representation	5,6
Constitution	11,12,13,14
Domestic Policy Agenda	5,8,9,15,17
Federalism	17,18
Foreign Policy	19,20
Interest Groups	8,9
Internal Security	6,7,9,10,11,12,13,15,16,18
Judicial Branch/Supreme Court	7,12,14
Mass Media	3,4
National Defense/Military	4
Policy Making Process	3,5,9
Political Culture	1,2
Political Parties and Partisanship	5,15
Presidency/Bush Administration/Executive Branch	1,2,5,11,14,18
Public Opinion	1,2
Separation of Powers	5,7,11
Technology and Politics	12,17,18

Introduction

It is no easy task accessing the impact upon the operation of American government of the September 11 terrorist attack on the Pentagon and World Trade Center. Despite general agreement that the assault on two of the main symbols of American political and economic power represents the most significant national event since Pearl Harbor six decades ago, what changes we are likely to see in the nation's politics beyond the short term remain speculative.

No definitive historical guidelines lend much specific insight into how the nation might react and adjust to September 11. Perhaps the Japanese attack on Pearl Harbor, a surprise attack by a foreign government that caused a significant loss of American life, represents the most parallel circumstance. But there are major differences between the two events. Pearl Harbor is now a distant memory, and most living Americans have no personal connection or intimate knowledge of the sneak attack. Unlike the air assault at Pearl Harbor, which occurred thousands of miles from American shores in a U.S. territory and was directed at military targets, the events of September 11 killed over 4,000 American civilians at work in two of the nation's most prominent cities. While reports of the Pearl Harbor attack trickled in by radio over the course of a few days in early December 1941, Americans experienced the events of September 11 almost as they happened via television. Japan was an identifiable enemy and the war against the Axis powers had the tangible goal of nothing less than the final surrender of our enemies. The war against terrorism is markedly different. This time the enemy is a mysterious, clandestine target, spread around the globe (with cells operating even within the United States). An end to the posed threat is difficult for public officials and citizens to envision. Indeed, some question whether or not "war" is even the appropriate word to describe military and domestic efforts to make the nation secure.

Still, beyond those immediately and directly affected by the September 11 tragedy, the terrorist attacks have already brought about changes in the lives of many Americans. Domestic security will never again be taken quite as much for granted. Government activity in regulating our lives has increased dramatically, from flying on airplanes to crossing the Canadian border to attending the Super Bowl. Overall, however, the short-run impact on ordinary citizens in the immediate aftermath of September 11 palls in comparison to that made after Pearl Harbor, when the nation prepared for a war perceived widely as a battle to save Western civilization. World War II mobilization affected all segments of American society and called for extensive personal sacrifices, including a military draft, the movement of women to the factory, and extensive rationing of many domestic, consumer goods ranging from sugar to automobile tires. Six months after September 11 the nation seems, at least outwardly, back to business as usual, with surprisingly little disruption to most people's lives.

But the September 11 attack has the potential to broadly affect politics, government, and in the end, the everyday lives of American citizens. Priorities on the national political agenda after the attack bear little resemblance to those before. As could be expected, increases in defense spending and internal security issues are now in the forefront. Issues that dominated the dialogue in the 2000 elections such as serious educational reform, easier access to prescription drugs for senior citizens, and protecting the Social Security Trust Fund, have been relegated to the backburner. The budget surplus of 2000 is quickly turning into a deficit, and increased defense and security expenses associated with fighting terrorism will only worsen budgetary matters. Debates over such issues, highly partisan in tone, are likely to reemerge at a later date if the terrorist threat diminishes. Other issues, however, may never regain their former importance. For example, national gun control efforts were stopped dead in their tracks for the foreseeable future. Had the hijackers used guns instead of box cutters as the weapons of choice, things would be very different.

Institutional power relationships have been disrupted in the aftermath of September 11 as well. The real question is whether or not the changed relationships are merely temporary or will become permanently engrained in the political system. In times of international crisis, Americans typically "rally around the flag," enhancing the power of the executive branch vis-à-vis both Congress and the judiciary. Presidential power expands in wartime, at least initially, as presidential approval ratings soar, providing the chief executive with an opportunity to take decisive action relatively unencumbered. Such was the case immediately after September 11: The polls revealed a massive increase in citizens' "trust in government," and Congress quickly pledged its bipartisan support for both the military effort in Afghanistan and President Bush's domestic security agenda. Perhaps the most controversial activities focused around the Justice Department's efforts to curb certain civil liberties in the name of national security. The courts eventually will have to deal with matters such as the intention of the federal government to challenge traditionally privileged communications between attorneys and their suspected terrorist clients; the lengthy detentions of suspects and witnesses without charges; and efforts to try suspected foreign terrorists by military tribunals that are beyond the scope of either congressional or judicial oversight.

Despite the appearance of dominance by a strong federal authority, American government in the aftermath of September 11 remains remarkably decentralized among various levels of authority. Even within levels, division and rivalry among bureaucratic agencies poses a problem for those seeking to mobilize resources for unified action. Homeland security, now perhaps the nation's highest priority, may prove to be the biggest challenge facing the U.S. political system. National security is no longer just about police and investigative agencies such as the FBI or the CIA, but about protecting citizens from such things as bio-terrorism and a disruption in the nation's agricultural production. Ex-Pennsylvania Governor Tom Ridge, President Bush's choice to head Homeland Security, faces a daunting task in trying to coordinate the anti-terrorism efforts of such diverse federal agencies as the Centers for Disease Control, the Federal Aviation Administration, the Postal Service Corporation, the Immigration and Naturalization service, and the Nuclear Regulatory Commission, to name just a few, as well as attempting to oversee the anti-terrorism efforts of state and local government officials. All of this takes place in the context of a diverse society designed to be open, with little control over borders or the movement of individuals within. Homeland security is as much about bureaucratic implementation as it is about the decisions of elected officials.

The articles selected for this book of readings have been chosen with an eye toward helping readers reflect on how American government and politics have been and will be affected by the events of September 11. This volume is envisioned to be a supplement to either an introductory American government textbook or book of readings. Of particular emphasis in this volume is how responding to the terrorist attacks represents a challenge to our governmental system. Many of the issues arising after September 11 remain unresolved and a matter of considerable conjecture. As a result, a number of the articles selected can be used in a debate format, revolving around such concerns as the role of the press in wartime, internal security vs. civil liberties, or whether or not tight homeland security is really possible in an open society.

The Context
After September 11

The Economist

What September 11th Really Wrought

America is getting back to normal after September 11th, partisan bickering and all. But the attacks may change politics in ways its politicians have not yet grasped

In one of the greatest political speeches, his second inaugural address, Abraham Lincoln argued that the civil war then raging was remaking American society despite the expectations and wishes of its leaders. "Neither party," he said, "expected for the war the magnitude or duration which it has already attained. Each looked for an easier triumph, and a result less fundamental and astounding."

Lincoln's equating of the difficulties of war with its consequences is telling. The civil war was momentous because it was traumatic. In contrast, the war against the Taliban has been "an easier triumph". Will it bring about "a result less fundamental"? September 11th ended America's decade-long "holiday from history."

The war in Afghanistan, of course, is only the beginning of the war against terror. No one knows how further attacks—by or against America—would affect the country. But already some changes are clear. September 11th ended what Charles Krauthammer, a columnist, mocked as a decade-long "holiday from history", when headlines were dominated by O.J. Simpson, Monica Lewinsky and Gary Condit (and, lest Britons feel smug, by Princess Diana). The new seriousness has shocked people out of that sense of fantasy.

More important, September 11th changed the non-trivial features of the 1990s, too. Back then, business, technology and communications mattered, but politics did not. Local issues meant more than national ones. Bill Gates and Jack Welch ranked as heroes, but government officials, from the president down, were villains, or near it.

In different ways, all these features were predicated on peace and prosperity. The prosperity was eroding even before September 11th, with the bursting of the dotcom bubble. The peace ended that day. As a result, personal insecurity was added to the mix. At a time when almost every indicator of well-being shows a "damn-the-terrorists" self-confidence, one measure points the other way. An increasing number of people say they think the future for their children got worse after September 11th. Americans used to believe that their mainland, at least, was invulnerable to outside attack, and felt secure accordingly. They no longer do.

The implications are profound. Politics will now become more important again, since the more people feel insecure, the more they will turn to the government for defence. This is a point that goes back to Thomas Hobbes (because the life of man is "nasty, brutish and short", people band together and create governments for self-protection). The most noticeable change to have occurred in America after September 11th is therefore not so surprising: a sharp rise in the level of public trust in the institutions of government.

In the mid-1960s, two-thirds of Americans said they trusted the federal government to do the right thing most or all of time—the highest rate in the world. By the mid-1990s, that figure had fallen to 20%, the lowest in any democracy. On September 11th, the figure more or less doubled overnight (see chart).

The scale of the change has been, to use Lincoln's term, astounding. The new trustfulness is felt on all sides, by Republicans and Democrats alike. Good opinions of the president, Congress, previously unknown cabinet officials and almost every institution of government have soared. Except in the case of the president himself, the rise in approval has been much larger than on any recent comparable occasion. "We're still too close to it, probably, to understand it all," the vice-president, Dick Cheney, told the Washington Post in late October. Still, he concluded, "it has altered the way the American people think about their government, and the role we have in society and overseas."

The persistence of trustfulness

The question is whether this level of trust will be sustained. If it were, it would affect America profoundly. In "The Confidence Gap" (1987), Bill Schneider and Seymour Martin Lipset argued that declining trust in government was the driving force of American politics in the 1970s and 1980s. It made Ronald Reagan's presidency possible, and Mr. Schneider has argued since that it encouraged others, notably Newt Gingrich, to give history a shove in the right direction by pruning back the functions of the state still further. If this nation-defining trend were reversed, it would presumably make possible a new round of government activism, comparable to one that took place during the cold war.

In the immediate aftermath of September 11th, such an interpretation seemed plausible. President George Bush won a large increase in federal spending to rebuild New York, compensate the families of victims and bail out airlines. He set up a new office of homeland security, the first such executive expansion for a decade, and agreed that the federal government should assume responsibility for airport security. John Ashcroft, the attorney-general, obtained expanded powers to monitor and detain terrorist suspects. The anthrax attacks ensured that the public health system would play a larger role against bioterrorism.

Yet, four months later, politics as normal is back. The parties are bickering about tax cuts (see article). Both sides are preparing to fight the 2002 elections on the economy, health care and education, issues that have dominated the agenda for years. Neither side expects the war to dampen partisan feelings. It is as if the attacks and the change in public sentiments never happened. Why?

For one thing, as Mr. Schneider points out, opinion polls held at moments of crisis should always be taken with a pinch of salt. Respondents interpret questions about trust in government as "Who do you support, your representatives or Osama bin Laden?" (Mr Bush's personal approval rating is boosted by the same phenomenon.) Moreover, the fact that the big rise in trust took place right after

September 11th—before the successes in Afghanistan—shows that it was driven not by popular acclaim for policies, but by a threatened nation rallying round the flag. As long as the sense of crisis remains, so will the level of trust. But, all things being equal, the two things are likely to fall in tandem. Already, the immediacy of the crisis is ebbing.

There is also evidence in the polls of public ambivalence towards government. When the Gallup organisation asked people whether they thought the government solved more problems than it created, it found the highest-ever proportion of respondents saying yes. But that was still only 42%, slightly smaller than the share which thinks the government creates more problems than it solves. When they asked people to rate the honesty of various professions, only a quarter gave members of Congress high marks, barely more than in 2000 (and far below the 90% rating for firemen and 84% for nurses in 2001). Even now, a narrow majority of Americans say they want a smaller government, providing fewer services. So, despite increased support for government at a general level, concerns about specific inefficiency or intrusiveness remain strong.

When all is said, the default setting for American politics is turned to "distrust", and only the biggest upheavals—civil war, depression, world war—can alter it profoundly. In his recent book, "The Strange Death of American Liberalism" (Yale, 2001), H.W. Brands argues that the expansion in the powers of government after the second world war was a historical anomaly. In the 1950s and 1960s, Americans defined themselves in opposition to the Soviet Union and its allies, and the occasional embarrassments of the comparison (America's treatment of blacks at home, for instance) drove politicians to enact the civil-rights legislation which expanded the federal government in the 1960s. When the ideological period of confrontation ceased and was replaced, with the start of détente, by traditional balance-of-power diplomacy, American politics began to revert to its distrustful mean, and the long slide in support for government began—exacerbated by defeat in Vietnam, Watergate and all the rest.

The war against terror, of course, is also a struggle of ideas rather than a territorial conflict. But this has never meant that it will have the same government-expanding effect as the cold war because, in one respect, it is quite different. Americans do not define themselves in contrast to terrorism in the same way as they did in opposition to communism. Mr. bin Laden's ideas seem too medieval and outlandish for direct comparison. Hence America's "asymmetric" conflict with small groups of terrorists is unlikely to have the same nation-defining quality as did the decades-long conflict between democratic and communist systems. The current high level of trust, therefore, is unlikely to be sustained. That, at least, is the politicians' view.

So far, all the examples of increased government activity have been in the area of national security itself or in sub-sectors of it (the airlines, for example). There is little evidence that the impetus to expand government is being carried beyond this. It is true that some mooted privatisations, of the Postal Service and of water-treatment plants around New Orleans, have been postponed. But these examples are few and far between, and would perhaps have happened anyway. It is also possible that, as recession takes its toll on local tax revenues, cities and states will be looking to save money over the next few years. If so, that would increase the pressure to privatise and shrink the role of the state.

Unchanging ways

Some Democrats had hoped that increased trust in government would translate into increased support for new entitlement programmes. The opposite seems to have happened. The "patients' bill of rights" (limiting the immunity of health maintenance organisations from being sued) had been high on the Democrats' agenda for this session of Congress. It is now dead. Debate may yet resume on a proposal to make prescription drugs available to old people through the government-funded Medicare system. But don't hold your breath: the proposal is costly, and federal dollars are more likely to go on defence. Gun sales have risen slightly, too, and new gun-control measures look unlikely. Paradoxically, then, one of the first effects of an attack that increased trust in government has been to destroy the most imminent proposals for increasing government's scope.

More broadly, if you compare domestic politics, the economy and foreign policy now with what they were like on September 10th, the striking thing is how little has changed, not how much. At home, politicians are reverting to partisan type, which could be significant: few things will do more to reduce trust in government than a year's worth of bickering.

On the economy, the terrorist attacks have not had the impact that was first feared. They did not cause the slowdown, of course (which had begun months before), nor did the response to them single-handedly destroy the federal budget surplus, which started to shrink in the summer. And although they may have deepened both, they do not seem likely to prolong the recession further than it would run anyway, at least if recent indicators are to be believed (the budget deficit is another matter).

On foreign policy, initial expectations of change have also been dashed. Europeans and many Democrats had hoped the war in Afghanistan would turn the Bush administration towards greater multi-lateralism. That has not happened. Although Colin Powell, the secretary of state, cobbled together an impressive anti-terrorist alliance, in Afghanistan itself the allied contribution was confined to providing air bases, overflight rights and British and Australian special forces. The war was conducted from day to day by Americans and Afghans, not by the wider coalition.

Subsequently, America has not engaged in the nation-building operations in Afghanistan, though it will provide the lion's share of money for rebuilding. And the administration has made good on its promise, made before September 11th, to withdraw from two arms-control treaties, abrogating the anti-ballistic missile (ABM) treaty and killing off the protocol to enforce the biological weapons convention.

This does not mean the administration has become hawkishly more unilateralist (remember that it has also been drawn back into diplomatic attempts to resolve disputes between the Palestinians and Israel and between India and Pakistan). Rather, the president and his men seem to be taking the high level of public support they now enjoy as a mandate for continuing with the foreign policy they had embarked upon anyway.

Shifts in the subsoil

In short, if you look at the immediate impact on America's current agenda, it seems modest. There is little support for a significant expansion in the scope of government (though, of course, plenty of argument over reordering priorities between, say, defence and social programmes). There are few signs that politicians think anything new is afoot. And the continuities of domestic, economic and foreign affairs seem more striking than the disruptions. So is the rising trust in government much ado about nothing?

Not quite. As Lincoln implied, wars change countries in ways that politicians do not necessarily expect or understand. They can set in motion events beyond anyone's control, for example raising expectations of government which demand to be met, or cause trouble if denied. Their impact is inherently unpredictable.

So it is worth asking whether American politicians may be misreading the signs of change. After all, less traumatic events than September 11th have changed the course of politics. The Oklahoma City bombing, for example, weakened Mr. Gingrich's anti-government revolution by showing federal employees as objects of sympathy. Has September 11th affected the subsoil of politics in such a way as to support bigger changes in future?

The answer is yes — or, at least, there are candidates for such changes. First, the attack seems to have altered the balance in America between security and civil liberties. Americans have acquiesced in Mr. Ashcroft's plans to boost the surveillance powers of law-enforcement officials and to make counter-terrorism the focus of the Justice Department. This is potentially a far-reaching change, confirming Alexander Hamilton's view that "to be more safe, [people] at length become willing to run the risk of being less free."

Second, the extremes of the political spectrum are likely to become less influential within the parties. The terrorist attacks cast a cloud of suspicion over all forms of religious certainty, and the fumbled response of the religious right has led many to disengage from politics altogether. On the left, the outpouring of patriotism, and the renewed focus on what holds Americans together, is likely to erode the influence of those who see the country largely as a coalition of ethnic subgroups and hyphenated-Americans. By eroding the influence of the two extremes — the most viscerally pro- and anti-government groups — September 11th may make incremental political change easier.

Third, the attacks may have the effect of explaining to Americans why they need to engage with the rest of the world on a sustained basis. So far, foreign policy has hardly changed, and the doctrine of seeking national security through military might understandably prevails. Yet the attacks on New York and Washington also showed that not even the world's largest defence budget can buy insulation from the world's demons any more. That, too, could have profound significance.

In short, this is a moment when American politics and the country's place in the world could be recast. The political class does not see it that way, and the eventual outcome will depend partly on the president. Franklin Roosevelt used the Depression to change Americans' relationship to their government. Harry Truman used the second world war to change their relationship with the rest of the world. It is not yet clear whether George Bush will be able to use the terrorist attacks to shape a comparable historic shift. But it is possible.

Shibley Telhami

Arab and Muslim America: A Snapshot

In a *New York Times* article appearing a week after the horror that befell America on September 11, a Muslim woman described her dilemma this way: "I am so used to thinking about myself as a New Yorker that it took me a few days to begin to see myself as a stranger might: a Muslim woman, an outsider, perhaps an enemy of the city. Before last week, I had thought of myself as a lawyer, a feminist, a wife, a sister, a friend, a woman on the street. Now I begin to see myself as a brown woman who bears a vague resemblance to the images of terrorists we see on television and in the newspapers. I can only imagine how much more difficult it is for men who look like Mohamed Atta or Osama bin Laden."

Excruciating moments like those the nation experienced last September test the identity of all Americans, but especially those whose identity may be caught in the middle. Many Arab and Muslim Americans lost loved ones and friends in the attacks in New York and Washington, and others had loved ones dispatched to Afghanistan as American soldiers to punish those who perpetrated the horror (Muslims are the largest minority religion in the U.S. armed forces). But many also had double fears for their own children. On the one hand, they shared the fears of all Americans about the new risks of terror; on the other, they were gripped by the haunting fear of their children being humiliated in school for who they are.

Two Partially Overlapping Communities

There is much that's misunderstood about Arabs and Muslims in America. Although the two communities share a great deal, they differ significantly in their make-up. Most Arabs in America are not Muslim,

Shibley Telhami, Anwar Sadat Professor at the University of Maryland, is a non-resident senior fellow in the Brookings Foreign Policy Studies Program.

and most Muslims are not Arabs. Most Arab Americans came from Lebanon and Syria, in several waves of immigration beginning at the outset of the 20th century. Most Muslim Americans are African American or from South Asia. Many of the early Arab immigrants assimilated well in American society. Arab-American organizations are fond of highlighting prominent Americans of at least partial Arab descent: Ralph Nader, George Mitchell, John Sununu, Donna Shalala, Spencer Abraham, Bobby Rahal, Doug Flutie, Jacques Nasser, Paul Anka, Frank Zappa, Paula Abdul, among many others. Like other ethnic groups in America, Arabs and Muslims have produced many successful Americans whose ethnic background is merely an afterthought.

Arab Americans now number more than 3 million, Muslims roughly 6 million (though estimates range from 3 million to 10 million). The income of Arab Americans is among the highest of any American ethnic group—second only to that of Jewish Americans. Arab Americans have become increasingly politicized over the years. According to a recent survey, proportionately more Arab Americans contribute to presidential candidates than any other ethnic group—and the groups surveyed included Asian Americans, Italian Americans, African Americans, Hispanic Americans, and Jewish Americans. Over the past decade especially, Arab-American political clout has increased. Although Arab Americans were long shunned by political candidates, President Clinton became the first sitting president to speak at conferences of Arab-American organizations, and both President Clinton and President Bush have normalized ongoing consultations with Arab- and Muslim-American leaders. In the fall 2000 election, presidential candidates sought the support of Arab Americans, not only for campaign contributions, but also as swing voters in key states, especially Michigan. The September 11 tragedy, coming just as Arab-American political clout was ascendant, has provided a real test for the community's role in American society and politics.

Impact of September 11

For Arab and Muslim leaders, the terrorist crisis has been like no other. It has forced them to contemplate profoundly their identity. Are they Arabs and Muslims living in America, or are they Americans with Arab and Muslim background? The answer came within hours after the terrorist attacks. Major Arab and Muslim organizations issued statements strongly condemning the attacks, refusing to allow their typical frustrations with issues of American policy in the Middle East to become linked to their rejection of the terror. Rarely have Arab and Muslim organizations in the United States been so assertive.

The enormity of the horror, the Middle Eastern background of the terrorists, and the terrorists' attempt to use religion to justify their acts have inevitably led to episodes of discrimination against Arabs and Muslims, as well as against those, such as Sikhs, who resemble them. But the support that both Arabs and Muslims received from thousands of people and organizations far outweighed the negative reaction. Arab and Muslim organizations were flooded with letters and calls of empathy from leaders and ordinary Americans, including many Jewish Americans, for most understood that at stake were the civil liberties of all Americans.

In large part, the public reaction was a product of quick decisions and statements by President Bush and members of his cabinet, members of Congress from both parties, and local political leaders. The president in particular acted quickly to make two central points that seem to have resonated with most of the public. The first was that the terrorists did not represent Islam and that Osama bin Laden must not be allowed to turn his terror into a conflict between Islam and the West. The second was that Muslim and Arab Americans are loyal Americans whose rights must be respected. Bush's early appearance at a Washington, D.C., mosque with Muslim-American leaders underlined the message.

The message seems to have gotten through. Despite the fears that many Americans now associate with people of Middle-Eastern background, a survey conducted in late October by Zogby International found that most Americans view the Muslim religion positively and that the vast majority of Arabs and Muslims approve the president's handling of the crisis. (Among Arab Americans, 83 percent give President Bush a positive performance rating.) Moreover, 69 percent of Arab Americans support "an all-out war against countries which harbor or aid terrorists."

Certainly, the events of September 11 will intensify the debate within the Arab and Muslim communities in America about who they are and what their priorities should be. One thing is already clear. Although both communities have asserted their American identity as never before and although 65 percent of Arab Americans feel embarrassed because the attacks were apparently committed by people from Arab countries, their pride in their heritage has not diminished. The

October survey found that 88 percent of Arab Americans are extremely proud of their heritage. So far, however, the terrorist attacks have not affected the priorities of the Arab public in America as might be expected, given Arab Americans' deep fear of discrimination.

Typically, Arab-American organizations highlight such domestic issues as secret evidence and racial profiling and such foreign policy issues as Jerusalem, Iraq, and the Palestinian-Israeli conflict. While Arab Americans, like other minorities, are involved in all American issues and are divided as Democrats and Republicans, as groups they inevitably focus on issues about which they tend to agree. The situation is no different from that of American Jews, who are also diverse, but whose organizations largely focus on issues of common interest.

Given the fear of profiling that Arab Americans had even before September, one would expect this issue to have become central for most of them since September 11. And for many it certainly has. Arab-American organizations, especially, have focused on it. But the findings of the Zogby poll among Arab Americans in October were surprising. Although 32 percent of Arab Americans reported having personally experienced discrimination in the past because of their ethnicity, and although 37 percent said they or their family members had experienced discrimination since September 11, 36 percent nevertheless supported profiling of Arab Americans, while 58 percent did not. Surprisingly, 54 percent of Arab Americans believed that law enforcement officials are justified in engaging in extra questioning and inspections of people with Middle Eastern accents or features.

Though their views on profiling have been mixed since September 11, Arab Americans have been considerably more unanimous on one subject—the need to resolve the Palestinian-Israeli dispute. Seventy-eight percent of those surveyed agreed that "a U.S. commitment to settle the Israeli-Palestinian dispute would help the president's efforts in the war against terrorism." Although most Arab Americans are Christian and mostly from Lebanon and Syria—and only a minority are Palestinians—their collective consciousness has been affected by the Palestinian issue in the same way that Arab consciousness in the Middle East has been affected. In a survey I commissioned in five Arab states (Lebanon, Syria, United Arab Emirates, Saudi Arabia, and Egypt) last spring, majorities in each country consistently ranked the Palestinian issue as "the single most important issue to them personally." The role of this issue in the collective consciousness of many Arabs and Muslims worldwide is akin to the role that Israel has come to play in contemporary Jewish identity.

Like all Americans since September 11, Arab and Muslim Americans are searching for solutions to terrorism. Like all Americans, they are also finding new meaning in aspects of their identity to which they might have given little thought a few short months ago.

II The Media

Robert J. Samuelson

Unwitting Accomplices?

The news media rank as one of the big winners of Sept. 11: Terrorism gave us a huge story and restored our seriousness of purpose. Because this good fortune seems almost indecent, hardly anyone mentions it. But before Sept. 11, the press was caught in a prolonged process of self-trivialization. We seemed to live in an era dominated by the personal, the small and the titillating. The summer's big stories were Gary Condit and shark attacks. Before that, there was Monica Lewinsky. Great national issues with heavy moral, political or social significance were disappearing, consigned to back pages or ignored altogether. Among media stars, many were enthusiastically self-absorbed, gleefully shrill and blissfully uninformed on matters of substance. Attitude was king or queen.

Now what we do has shifted dramatically. Here is a story that truly matters. It's about good and evil, life and death, war and peace, religion, technology, the clash of cultures—our future as a society.

Suddenly, we are no longer focused obsessively on the latest sex scandal. Substance counts. We need science reporters to distinguish between a microbe and a molecule, defense reporters to explain B-2s, and foreign correspondents to interpret various Islamic sects that—until a few weeks ago—were unknown to most Americans. The story is thrilling, and people thirst for it. Great.

However, journalistic hazards lurk. The most obvious and, in my view, the least worrisome is the danger of becoming a propaganda arm for the government—passive, uncritical and gullible. Of course no one should expect the news media to be neutral. Are we supposed to be indifferent to the outcome? As ordinary Americans, reporters, editors and their families are as vulnerable to terrorism as anyone else. And news organizations are special targets.

But just because our sympathies are clear doesn't mean we've lost our skepticism. Already, papers and TV news programs are filled with stories suggesting that the "war on terrorism" is going badly and that the Pentagon, the CIA and the FBI don't know what they're doing. For better or worse, modern journalism is reflexively skeptical of government officials (though not necessarily of government). Vietnam and Watergate have left their marks. The other safeguard against parochialism is the war's international character. Coverage is global; foreign media—monitored by our own media—ensure different perspectives.

The greater danger, I suspect, is just the opposite. It is that our new obsession with terrorism will make us its unwitting accomplices. We will become (and have already partly become) merchants of fear. Case in point: the anthrax fright. Until now, anthrax has been a trivial threat to public health and safety: four people have died of the 17 known to have been infected. So far, it's the functional equivalent of a mad gunman on the loose or a biological Unabomber. By contrast, there were 42,000 deaths from car accidents and 17,000 from homicides in 1998.

Yet, the news media have treated anthrax as a lurking scourge that might quickly strike all. I understand the causes of this: the closeness of Sept. 11; the fact that it's in the mail system; its appearance at highly visible places (Congress, the Supreme Court, news organizations); the speed with which it kills, if inhaled; the fear of the unknown and the specter of a broader attack. Still, the coverage has so far been all out of proportion to the actual threat.

No self-respecting editor wants to be accused—after some future terrorist act—of not having pointed out the obvious risks beforehand. Sensationalism seems justified. The ensuing explosion of stories has highlighted our multiple vulnerabilities: to chemical, biological and nuclear devices; or at airports, reservoirs, stadiums and nuclear plants. Similarly, no public figure wants to be crucified for having concealed warnings of terrorist attacks if the attacks actually occur, because the warnings would almost certainly be revealed. On its simplest level, this is why we've had two warnings from the Bush administration against unspecified terrorist threats and one from California Gov. Gray Davis about threats to the state's bridges. Public officials and the news media both have understandable incentives to be alarmist.

The perverse result is that we may become the terrorists' silent allies. Terrorism is not just about death and destruction. It's also about creating fear, sowing suspicion, undermining confidence in public leadership, provoking people—and governments—into doing things that they might not otherwise do. It is an assault as much on our psychology as on our bodies.

Let me admit: I have no superior insight about where and how to draw the line. Because what happened on Sept. 11 was so unimaginable, almost any threat—no matter how implausible it once seemed—now seems conceivable. But I do know that the sort of saturation coverage that we're now getting may create false fears and false expectations. It may take years to find the source of anthrax; the Unabomber was caught almost two decades after his first bomb, and not until he was turned in by his brother. Nor can we protect ourselves against every possible threat. But exaggerated fears may stimulate hoaxes or convert minor terrorist acts into large public events.

The fate of the war against terrorism will be determined more by the nation's ability to roll up terrorist networks and prevent the spread of weapons of mass destruction than by our ability to fortify every potential target against every potential danger. The effort to do that could prove enormously costly and disruptive of everyday life without, in the end, actually improving our security. Pursuing this important story, we media types need to recognize that our very zealousness makes us part of the story and, possibly, not for the good.

Stuart Taylor Jr.

Legal Affairs:
The Media, the Military, and
Striking the Right Balance

This war will severely test the inherently uneasy relationship between the government—especially the military—and the media. The chafing has already begun. While the Bush Administration so far seems largely to have avoided the outright deceptions practiced by its predecessors, it has exhibited an unhealthy impulse to control the news by leaning on the media not to publish enemy "propaganda." And while much of the news coverage has been superb, some journalists have exhibited a reckless indifference to endangering military operations and the lives of our soldiers, and a reflexive hostility toward the military. The military and the Administration have ample reason to distrust some reporters and editors

If we are going to get this right, the government must not resort unnecessarily to secrecy or to lightly tarring independent journalists as disloyal. The media should not frivolously cry "censorship." And each should work harder to understand the views and accommodate the needs of the other.

The delicacy of the task is exemplified by the Administration's requests that the media filter public statements by Osama bin Laden and his fellow mass murderers before airing them. National Security Adviser Condoleezza Rice took a small but worrisome step down a slippery slope when she urged network executives not to broadcast bin Laden videos without first reviewing and editing them down to brief excerpts. Although her warning that bin Laden might be sending coded messages in Arabic to operatives planning new attacks was plausible, any such messages could almost as easily be sent through foreign networks, the Internet, or the mail. And while Rice's more emphatic concern about indiscriminate airing of enemy propaganda was understandable, some such propaganda is undeniably newsworthy. White

Stuart Taylor Jr. is a senior writer for *National Journal* magazine, where "Opening Argument" appears.

House Press Secretary Ari Fleischer clumsily lurched farther down the same slope when he urged newspapers not to publish full transcripts of enemy rants. His suggestion that terrorists would look to printed English-language translations for coded marching orders was as far-fetched as his notion that little-read transcripts could be an effective propaganda vehicle.

Such official efforts to influence editorial discretion are fraught with danger, likely to be futile, and sometimes self-defeating. Fraught with danger because when the government is talking, it is but a short step from making reasoned critiques to questioning the loyalty of reporters and editors. Futile because bin Laden's propaganda has little impact outside the Muslim world, where people will watch unedited bin Laden videos elsewhere if CNN does not show them. Self-defeating because the videos are the best public evidence by far of bin Laden's role in the September 11 mass murders and his moral depravity.

Similarly ill-advised was the State Department's pressure on the government-funded Voice of America radio to shelve an interview with Taliban leader Mullah Mohammed Omar. The VOA's hard-won reputation for balanced and independent news coverage accounts for its remarkable following in Afghanistan, where surveys show that 67 percent of all men tune in daily. If it becomes a one-sided official mouthpiece, skeptical listeners will switch to the BBC or the virulently anti-American tirades that pervade most other broadcasts in the Middle East.

History provides ample reason for *Washington Post* columnist E.J. Dionne's view that "the coming struggles between the government and the media over the public's right to know will have less to do with protecting individuals and operations than officials may argue. All governments have an interest in shielding themselves from reports of failure. The easiest alibi for cover-ups is to claim that the truth is dangerous." But the military and the Administration also have ample reasons to distrust some reporters and editors.

Dionne confidently claims that "no reporter I know" wants to be responsible for "blowing the cover of individuals or military operations." Perhaps he does not know Loren Jenkins, senior foreign editor of National Public Radio, who explained his ethical principles to *The Chicago Tribune*: "Asked whether his team [of reporters] would report the presence of an American commando unit found in, say, a northern Pakistan village, [Jenkins] doesn't exhibit any of the hesitation of some of his news-business colleagues, who stress that they try to factor security issues into their coverage decisions. 'You report it,' Jenkins says. 'I don't represent the government. I represent history, information, what happened.'"

Of course, "what happens" might well be influenced—and American operations and lives endangered—by the kind of reporting that Jenkins vows to do. Are he and NPR aberrants? Well, consider a televised 1987 roundtable discussion among some military men and two famous journalists. The hypothetical question for the journalists was what they would do if, after accepting (as both said they would) an invitation to travel behind enemy lines, they found themselves with an enemy unit preparing to ambush unsuspecting American and allied soldiers. Peter Jennings said with evident ambivalence that he would do his best to warn the Americans. But then, Mike Wallace asserted without hesitation that good reporters (clearly including him) "would regard it simply as another story they were there to cover." He berated Jennings and rejected the moderator's suggestion that he might have some higher duty than filming the slaughter of his countrymen: "No. You don't have a higher duty. No. No. You're a reporter!" Whereupon Jennings, embarrassed by his lapse into human decency, reversed himself and agreed with Wallace.

The military men were horrified. "What's it worth?" a former general (Brent Scowcroft) bitterly demanded of Wallace. "It's worth 30 seconds on the evening news, as opposed to saving a platoon." Marine Colonel George M. Connell spat out a more concise reaction: "I . . . feel . . . utter . . . contempt." Amen. All this gives a hollow ring to former television correspondent Marvin Kalb's assertion, in an op-ed in *The New York Times*, that the Administration "must recognize that in this fight the press . . . is a valuable and necessary ally, if treated with . . . trust." This is the same Kalb who had previously mused in another op-ed, in *The Washington Post*: "Certain operations are to be super secret. If a reporter learns about one, should he report it? . . . And if he doesn't report it and the operation turns out to be badly conceived and costly in casualties, does his reticence serve his profession or his country? To these questions, there are no easy answers, no glib guidelines."

Here's an easy guideline: No decent journalist, no decent American, would ever risk endangering the lives of American soldiers or—in this of all wars—the secrecy of military operations for something as petty and self-serving as a lousy little scoop. Or, for that matter, a great big scoop. Kalb's implication that reporters with access to fragmentary leaks are better qualified than military commanders to judge whether secret operations are "badly conceived" is breathtaking in its arrogance. (Full disclosure: Kalb has been critical of my own work.)

Jenkins, Wallace, Jennings, and Kalb exemplify a mind-set that holds that beating the competition even to stories that would soon become public anyway or that smack more of sensationalism than of educating the public is so transcendent a value as to justify virtual indifference to any harm that journalists might cause (or fail to prevent). If you were a military commander, would you want to help people like these get close to ground operations in Afghanistan, secret or otherwise? Would Jenkins's assertion (to *The Tribune*) that military officials "never tell you the truth" instill confidence in his own trustworthiness and fairness?

This is not to suggest that the Administration and the military should slam the doors in the face of all reporters. Most, or at least many, can be trusted. And keeping the media at a greater distance from combat operations than security requires would contribute to a bitterly adversarial military-media relationship. This, in turn, would likely hurt the war effort in the long run by inviting relentlessly negative coverage and fanning public distrust. Nor is this to deny that the media's most vital mission — keeping the government honest — requires both healthy skepticism and the fortitude to dig out and publish bad news, even in the face of official and public wrath.

Sometimes, as in the 1971 Pentagon Papers case, good journalism also calls for publishing important news in the face of transparently unwarranted stamps of official secrecy and attempted official censorship.

But in assessing alleged security risks, the media should give due weight to the fact that the officials often have more complete information and far, far more grave responsibilities. We cannot and should not recreate the uncritical media cheerleading of the World War II era. But we must avoid the corrosive military-media hostility that started in Vietnam and has since been fed both by official deceptions and by the mindless anti-military bias inculcated in many of us by our college professors. This war — unlike Vietnam — really does pit good against evil, civilization against barbarism, life and liberty against nihilism. Journalistic neutrality is not a tenable stance.

III Government Institutions

Sarah Binder and Bill Frenzel

The Business of Congress After September 11: A Look Back and at What's Ahead for 2002

Policy Dialogue #1 — January 2002

The terrorist attacks on September 11, which caused plane crashes in New York, Pennsylvania, and Washington, D.C., resulted in thousands of deaths, billions of dollars in damage, and an American public that was stunned by the events it had watched unfold on television. In addition to the heavy emotional toll, federal, state, and local governments scrambled to address new policy problems, including massive clean—up efforts, compensation for victims, and homeland security.

How did Congress address the immediate crisis and move forward in the days and months that followed? How will the events of September 11 continue to influence the congressional agenda in the second session? The Brookings Institution asked two of its scholars — congressional expert Sarah Binder and former Congressman Bill Frenzel — to discuss how the 107th Congress dealt with the effects of the attacks in the days immediately following September 11, how lawmakers balanced the emergency with other pending legislation, and what the public can expect from Congress in the first months of the second session.

Q. Is there any historic precedent for how the terrorist attacks of September 11 have focused Congress so intently on one major issue that needs so much money and attention?

Sarah Binder: The only event that comes close to approaching September 11 in terms of its impact on Congress and the nation is the 1941 bombing of Pearl Harbor, but it is difficult to compare the current Congress with the ones that met during World War II. For one thing, today's partisan environment bears little resemblance to the 1930s and early 1940s. When President [Franklin D.] Roosevelt faced the Congress, he had the advantage of leading a House and Senate controlled by his own party by very large margins. Today, President Bush must work with a House that his party controls by the slimmest of margins, and a Senate controlled by Democrats. Today's divided government poses a challenge for a wartime president that FDR never had to face.

Sarah Binder is a fellow in Governmental Studies at the Brookings Institution, an associate professor of political science at George Washington University, and the former press secretary and legislative aide to U.S. Representative Lee H. Hamilton (D—Ind.). She is the co-author of *Politics or Principle? Filibustering in the United States Senate* and the author of *Minority Rights, Majority Rule: Partisanship and the Development of Congress.*

Bill Frenzel is a guest scholar in Governmental Studies at the Brookings Institution and a former member of the U.S. House of Representatives (R-Minn., 1971-1991). He is a member of the bipartisan commission on Social Security convened by President George W. Bush in 2001.

Bill Frenzel: When I was a congressman, there was nothing that commanded the level of attention that September 11 did. I started my congressional career when Vietnam was winding down, and the other significant crises that took place while I was in office—the hostages in Iran, the run-up to the Gulf War—paled in comparison to what we saw this fall. In fact, as Sarah said, only Pearl Harbor was comparable in terms of the level and impact of devastation.

Q. But haven't there been other changes in American government and society that make the situation after September 11, 2001, different from the situation after December 7, 1941?

Binder: Sure. The context in which legislators and the president meet to conduct business differs considerably from the legislative environment of the 1930s and 1940s. The legislative agenda was much smaller than the one we see today, as America had experienced neither the momentous wartime growth of the federal government nor the mammoth expansion of federal programs that occurred during the Great Society congresses of the 1960s. So it was much easier for Congress to focus on wartime legislative proposals, as legislators were sacrificing little of whatever personal or partisan legislative agendas they may have held. The events of September 11, on the other hand, radically shifted the congressional agenda, causing numerous pending social and economic proposals to stall.

Q. In what other ways is the post-September 11 world different from the post-December 7 world?

Binder: We can draw some interesting comparisons between the day-to-day business of Congress during the two war periods. First, both presidents enjoyed very strong public support, bolstering their position in facing the Congress. Today, there is essentially no domestic political opposition to the war against terrorism and the administration's agenda of destroying the al Qaeda network. And although there may have been some early opposition to FDR from isolationists resisting international entanglements, any domestic opposition basically ended when Americans were attacked at home by the Japanese assault on Pearl Harbor.

Frenzel: That's a good point about public support. After September 11, both parties knew what the American people wanted and tried to deliver it. The airline bailout legislation, for example, was quickly drawn and obviously flawed. Absent an emergency, there would have been heated debate, many amendments, and an uncertain outcome. But the fact was that the airlines were in big trouble, and lawmakers had to do something about it. In periods of crisis, legislation that is less than perfect tends to move quickly. As a lawmaker, when you pass bills in an emergency, you know you're going to make mistakes. The reality is that the emergency warrants quick and sometimes imperfect work, but it is more important to get bills passed in order to help the nation move forward.

Q. Let's examine some of the specifics. The agenda confronting Congress changed drastically on September 11, didn't it?

Frenzel: You bet it did. Contentious issues—campaign finance reform, a patients' bill of rights, and changes to Medicare benefits—were moved to the back burner while emergency issues such as disaster relief, an airline bailout, airport security, and homeland security enforcement powers were given immediate priority. In an emergency, the Congress can move swiftly, and it did. The normal diversions that add so much time to the legislative process—including budget restrictions, partisanship, parochialism, and members' philosophical leanings—were not ignored, but they were reduced. The emergency issues were generally given low-decibel, modest debate, and dispatched promptly.

Q: When the nation is facing a threat like the current one, does Congress generally concede to all of the president's requests?

Binder: After September 11, Congress acquiesced quickly to President Bush's demands for financial support for New York and for the airline industry, but it did not completely give in to his requests. Congress refused, for example, to give the administration a blank check and authority over how appropriated funds would be spent. But in comparison to the partisan deadlock that often arose before September 11, Congress made a concerted effort to ensure swift legislative action on the president's requests. When little domestic opposition exists, legislators have considerable leeway to defer to the president's wartime agenda, even if they differ over the ways and means of responding to the crisis itself. Other big issues on the agenda, as a consequence, get side-tracked, many even evaporating from legislators' active agendas, as Bill suggested. The summer preoccupations with a Social Security "lockbox," prescription drug benefits, and the rights of managed care patients all but disappeared after September 11. Much of this is because the events of that day command far greater attention than domestic priorities. But it is also the consequence of a rapidly deteriorating economy and the war on terrorism's need for dwindling federal dollars.

The same atmosphere prevailed in the 1940s, when few members of Congress wanted to be viewed as obstructing the president's ability to prosecute a war. In fact, Congress approved a series of war powers acts in the early 1940s intended to delegate considerable economic powers to the president and the administration. But just as today's Congress has not completely deferred to the president's preferences, lawmakers in the 1940s occasionally challenged FDR. The further Roosevelt's legislative requests strayed from the war effort, the more resistance he encountered from an increasingly fractured Democratic party. For example, although FDR eventually prevailed, he met with concerted opposition to a series of economic stabilization measures. Likewise, Democrats today have been willing to challenge the president on measures not directly tied to the war effort, as seen in the unfinished battle over an economic stimulus bill. The bill passed the House, but stalled in the Senate because the two parties disagree over the right way to bolster a failing economy. With control of both chambers at stake in the upcoming midterm elections, Bush's popularity alone is unlikely to convince Democrats to concede to the Republican plan.

Frenzel: The contentious issues moved to the back end of the line after September 11. They are not dead, and will probably return in 2002. Other issues that were moving toward consensus or in which both parties had made heavy political investments, like education reform and election procedural reform, kept moving forward. The education reauthorization bill passed and election reform legislation will probably pass in the first half of 2002. Both parties saw virtue and political benefit in each of those bills and perhaps felt pressure from their constituents to finish work on them.

What happened to appropriations bills and budget limitations was not as pretty. Once September 11 swept away the last of the budget restraints of the 1990 Budget Enforcement Act, the congressional urge to spend ballooned. The myth of the Social Security "lockbox" was shattered; discretionary spending will increase about 8.5 percent; and baselines will continue to escalate. The major damage to the budget was done by the September 11 attack and the economy, but Congress was quick to pile on.

Q: How do you think Congress did this past fall in terms of putting aside their differences to move legislation?

Binder: I think it's safe to say that Congress got very high marks for its bipartisan behavior following the September 11 attacks. By all accounts, the leadership of the two parties worked in concert with President Bush to address his initial request for financial aid. Less noticed, perhaps — but no less important — was Congress's ability to act "bicamerally," if you will. Although differences between the House and Senate have often killed major issues in recent years, including prescription drug coverage and a patients' bill of rights, no such bicameral roadblocks emerged this time around.

Frenzel: In a national emergency, the country is drawn together. Congress, which is both representative and highly sensitive, was able to respond immediately and almost unanimously to the events of September 11. Polls showed the public approved of both Congress' attitude and response. After that, bipartisanship and the general feeling of unity in Congress began to wane. As public fears of further terrorist actions abated, the pressures on Congress to act together declined. Instead, pressures driven by party differences and by what are expected to be close elections in 2002 began to move the House and Senate back to their normal, competitive mode. By the time Congress adjourned in December, little unity remained. If the war on terrorism goes badly, or if most Americans fear that more attacks at home are likely, congressional unity will return. If not, the law of the jungle will prevail.

Binder: What is striking about this initial bipartisanship was how different it was from the president's style of building bipartisan coalitions early in his administration before the terrorist attacks. In building these coalitions (for instance, on the tax cut enacted last spring), Bush reached out primarily to centrist Democrats to build a winning coalition with his Republican base. He did not, however, reach out to the Democratic leadership — what some would refer to as a preferred path for building truly bipartisan solutions. After September 11, Bush met weekly with House and Senate leaders from both parties. So in giving high marks to the Congress for its bipartisanship, it's important to recognize how the president's procedural tactics made such bipartisanship possible.

Not every measure proposed by the administration in response to the attacks, however, sailed so easily through the two parties and chambers. Aviation security and anti-terrorism bills elicited much greater opposition and conflict, although both were eventually signed into law. Interestingly, conflict over these measures grew along several different dimensions. Disagreements over the aviation security bill were as much between the House and Senate as between Republicans and Democrats—the president expressing only limited support for the positions maintained by his House Republican base. Anti-terrorism measures also attracted considerable debate, with some Republicans on the right agreeing with Democrats on the left that the enhanced powers requested for the Justice Department intruded too much on citizens' civil liberties. In each of these cases, however, negotiators were able to reach final agreement with the president. The president was sufficiently flexible on his priorities and Congress was unwilling to be seen as obstructing him on legislative measures directly related to the attacks.

Q: Now that the immediate shock and political unity that followed September 11 is wearing off somewhat, what do you expect during the second session of Congress that's just beginning?

Frenzel: The second session of the 107th Congress will be more like the period before September 11 than the period between September 11 and Thanksgiving. The forces that drive the parties apart have now become stronger than the unifying forces. The closer Congress gets to the elections, the more aggressive both parties will become. Issues will also be more contentious as the parties strive to emphasize their differences, rather than their similarities.

Binder: I certainly agree with Bill on that. I'm skeptical as to whether this bipartisan and bicameral effectiveness will continue in the second session, for a number of reasons. First, in spite of September 11, all the ingredients that encouraged legislators to deadlock on major issues in the early months of the Bush administration are still in place. We still see very polarized political parties that hold extremely slim margins of leadership in each chamber, making it especially difficult for Bush and the Republicans to build the large bipartisan coalitions necessary for reaching major policy agreements. We see strong differences between the House and Senate on a number of issues, including preferred measures for addressing patients' rights, energy development and conservation, and faith-based initiatives. And we see the slimmest of Senate margins, a condition that makes it especially difficult to build cloture-proof, 60-vote majorities. Democrats are already willing to stand up to the president on measures unrelated to the war effort, and even on issues spurred by the war effort, like the economic stimulus bill. Democrats dug in against tax cut provisions preferred by the president and congressional Republicans.

Frenzel: In 2002, we'll see Congress revert to its normal rhythms. But Congress will be in or close to (depending on the fiscal stimulus) a deficit situation for fiscal 2002 and 2003. The economy has taken a severe hit, and its recovery, or lack thereof, will have a strong influence on the way Congress operates. The president's budget must be presented early in the year, when there is insufficient information available about a potential recovery. Congress' spending binge of discretionary increases of 10 percent in fiscal 2001 and 8.5 percent (before supplemental appropriations) in FY02 has already swollen spending baselines. Absent a strong, fast recovery, the fiscal 2003 budget could make lawmakers' lives even more unpleasant than might even be expected in a year of close congressional elections. Absent more domestic terrorism, we can expect a contentious second session.

Binder: The economic context has certainly shifted radically since September. The year began with projections of huge budget surpluses, but today we find ourselves likely facing budget deficits for the duration of the Bush administration. To be sure, partisans differ over the causes of the emerging deficits. Some fault the president's tax cuts this past spring; others point to the impact of September 11 on the economy and the diversion of funds to war and recovery efforts. Regardless of the cause, we are no longer facing an ever-expanding federal treasury that would have provided ample funds for the major domestic initiatives that had been on the agenda before September 11. Even if there were the political will to return to issues such as prescription drug coverage and managed care reform, the new economic context likely makes enacting these programs prohibitively expensive.

I don't think, though, that all major issues will end in gridlock in the second session. The legislative horizon is not that bleak, although a lot will depend on Bush's domestic agenda for 2002. And that, of course, depends equally on the progress and direction of the war efforts in the interim. Both parties retain an incentive to meet public demands on major issues, as evidenced by the successful effort to reach final agreement in December on the president's education reform bill.

Q: You seem to feel that public pressure may keep Congress from falling back into partisanship and deadlock even after some of the unifying effects of September 11 fade away.

Binder: My view is that public pressures for action must compete with the political parties' differing views on how best to approach these measures. And so long as the economy remains sluggish and deficits are projected to rise, it will be extremely difficult for legislators and the president to agree on major policy changes—even if events are not overshadowed by the war against terrorism. I also think it's important to keep in mind sheer human limits in speculating about the agenda of the second session. Part of the reason domestic issues have taken a back seat to the war effort is simply that so many people can only work on so many issues at one time. Not only is the president's attention diverted by the war away from domestic issues, but his time is diverted as well. Another important consideration is that central to forwarding the president's agenda before September 11 had been Vice President Cheney, who is now deeply involved in the war effort.

Frenzel: Well, my view is that last September and October, lawmakers were unified in supporting the war on terrorism and were satisfied to temporarily set aside other issues. But by November, the perception of the urgency of the war had eroded somewhat. Its willingness to adjourn in December without passing an economic stimulus bill, for example, would have been unthinkable in September. A unified Congress will continue to support the war, but as soon as the war seems less urgent, the political forces that tend to divide the Congress will get stronger. Both parties will give their domestic agendas higher priority. Those members who oppose the president's domestic policies will do so openly, while at the same time supporting him on the conduct and the costs of the war.

Q: Do you think the war on terrorism imposes special responsibilities on Congress to act in a more cooperative, less confrontational way when dealing with the president and his agenda?

Binder: There's no single, correct answer to that question. Reasonable people can differ on the appropriate role of Congress during wartime, just as they might differ on Congress's responsibilities when the nation is not at war. What we want to know, of course, is just what kind of balance Congress should strike in its relationship with the president. Certainly the Congress should not excessively defer to the president to the point that it loses its ability to serve as a constitutional check on the actions of the executive. But neither would most of us want to have a Congress that refuses to accede to the preferences of the president in times of dire emergency.

The constitutional character of the Congress—with 535 independent voices—is simply not equipped to act uniformly and with dispatch in times of real trouble. The challenge for Congress is to determine the appropriate balance of power between the branches. Interestingly, Congress has throughout its history oscillated between poles of deference and independence, shifting its authority over time. Congress wrote the president a blank check in 1964 when it passed the Tonkin Gulf resolution during the Vietnam conflict, but years later found itself trying to rein in the excesses of an "imperial" presidency. That our institutions are not rigidly fixed probably helps account for the resiliency of our political system.

Frenzel: In the fall of 1990, during the time leading up to the Gulf War, Congress was engaged in negotiations over the budget. Members were aggressive in their opposition to President [George H.W.] Bush's domestic program. At the same time, lawmakers knew that Bush needed the money for the Gulf War and so they didn't hold back in that regard. However, their support was not as unified or vigorous as it has been during the current debates over military action in Afghanistan.

Overall, though, members of Congress generally will not reserve all criticism of the president during a crisis. They may hold off for awhile, as they did in the aftermath of September 11, but ultimately partisanship returns. If other incidents occurred that reinforced the unified feeling of the American public in the way that September 11 did, then Congress' own unity may be restored, if temporarily.

Binder: No matter who controls the national agenda, there are signs that considerable authority and discretion have already shifted back to the executive in the aftermath of September 11. Congress has enacted (and in the case of military tribunals, the president has claimed) considerable powers for detaining and prosecuting suspected terrorists. We have also seen various agencies such as the CIA and the FBI reorient their priorities around fighting terrorism. As long as the president can claim that national security demands that policymakers dedicate time and resources to fighting terrorism, it may be difficult for Congress to shift the nation's attention and resources back to the domestic arena. The reappearance of budget deficits will also constrain legislators seeking to return to the agenda prevailing before the terrible events of September.

Frenzel: Another incident that focused the nation's attention during my time in office was the 1979-1980 hostage crisis in Iran. Not only were Republicans unhappy with the way President Carter handled it, but they used it as an election issue against him. Again, this was not an event that had the overwhelming impact that September 11 did on Congress and the country, but members were not afraid to openly criticize the president about it.

For members of Congress beginning the second session, the war goes on, but the full emergency wartime status was lifted before 2001 ended. That means members will be more vocal in their criticism of the president's domestic policies than they were this fall.

Binder: Even if there is a political or institutional will to challenge the president's control of the agenda, economic constraints may limit Congress's ability to do much about it. That may be the most enduring consequence of September 11 for the business of Congress.

Legislation on Terrorism

Before the first session of the 107th Congress adjourned in December, lawmakers cleared nine bills and three joint resolutions related to the September 11 terrorist attacks. Congress also approved ten other resolutions, which are not signed by the president and do not have the force of law, and introduced roughly 200 bills or resolutions that saw some or no action. The following terrorism-related bills and joint resolutions were signed into law by President George W. Bush following Sept. 11:

H.R. 2882: Public Safety Officer Benefits bill

H.R. 2883: Intelligence Authorization Act, FY02

H.R. 2888: 2001 Emergency Supplemental Appropriations Act

H.R. 2926: Air Transportation Safety and System Stabilization Act

H.R. 3162: Uniting and Strengthening America by Providing Appropriate Tools Required to Intercept and Obstruct Terrorism (USA PATRIOT) Act of 2001

H.J. Res. 71: Designating Sept. 11 as Patriot Day

S. 1424: Amending Immigration and Nationality Act to provide permanent authority for the admission of "S" visa non-immigrants

S. 1438: Defense Authorization Act, FY02

S. 1447: Aviation and Transportation Security Act

S. 1465: A bill to authorize the president to exercise waivers of foreign assistance restrictions with respect to Pakistan through Sept. 30, 2003, and for other purposes

S.J. Res. 22: Joint resolution expressing the sense of Congress regarding the terrorist attacks

S.J. Res. 23: Authorization for Use of Military Force

Source: THOMAS, as of Jan. 14, 2002.

Norman J. Ornstein

Can Congress Recover from 9/11?

Ever since September 11 the executive branch has been front and center on America's political stage. The president, once caricatured for quitting work at five o'clock and spending more time at his ranch than at the White House, is now viewed almost universally as the leader of the free world. Donald Rumsfeld and Colin Powell are media superstars. Even the more obscure cabinet secretaries, like Norm Mineta and Tommy Thompson, have become near-celebrities.

The legislative branch, by contrast, has largely receded into the background. As recently as this past summer, it was Congress that was setting the agenda in Washington. (Remember the patients' bill of rights?) But since the terrorist attacks, Capitol Hill has largely followed the White House's lead—passing the president's education and anti-terror legislation, granting him trade promotion authority, and ultimately abandoning an economic stimulus package when the president didn't like the Senate's ideas. But Congress has receded in an even more fundamental way in the past several months. Long celebrated as the most open political institution in the world, Congress has become cut off from the public. Members have traditionally maintained a close connection to constituents through the immediate turnaround of mail, and

Norman J. Ornstein is a resident scholar at AEI.

regular, face-to-face contact with voters both at the Capitol and back home in their districts. But since September 11 these connections have all become increasingly tenuous.

Consider the postal situation on Capitol Hill. Answering mail is at the core of operations for every member of Congress. At least half of the 11,200 staffers on Capitol Hill spend time on constituent mail—processing, organizing, cataloguing, writing and sending responses. Virtually all members of Congress have prided themselves on their quick mail turnaround, answering most constituents in a matter of hours or days. The first piece of advice given to freshmen, especially those from shaky or ideologically incompatible districts, is to get the mail operation in shape; constituents will forgive a lot of errant votes if they think their lawmakers are responsive to their individual needs or demands.

But since the terrorist attacks—and especially since the anthrax-laden letter sent to Senator Tom Daschle—the mail service for Congress has been frozen in place. According to estimates, more than 300,000 pieces of mail to members of Congress have been quarantined, awaiting irradiation. Many of the people who wrote these letters have no idea why they haven't received a reply. What little mail has trickled into congressional offices, one House member told me over the holidays, "has been so irradiated it literally crumbles in your hands."

Even when all the mail is ultimately delivered, it's unclear what many senators will be able to do with it: The Hart Senate Office Building, home to 50 of the 100 senators, has been shuttered because of the anthrax letter, leaving legislators and their staffs homeless, often crowding into small committee spaces, Capitol hideaways, and the offices of accommodating colleagues in the other two Senate office buildings. Iowa Senator Charles Grassley, the powerful senior Republican on the Finance Committee, has been forced to send his staff to five separate locations, including the conference room of Illinois Senator Peter Fitzgerald and a postal annex blocks from the Capitol. Majority Leader Tom Daschle has said that it's possible the Hart refugees will be able to return to their building later this month. "I can only hope we'll have some time before Congress starts up with the budget and terrorism to get moved back, organized, and get out from under," laments one staffer.

Then there's the matter of human traffic. According to the Capitol Preservation Commission, some 4 million people visit the Capitol every year, many of them American tourists and schoolchildren—voters and voters-to-be who can see the legislative process in action and make a direct connection to their members of Congress. Before visitors can sit in the galleries and watch the House or Senate in action, they must obtain gallery passes, which Congress cleverly makes available only at their representatives' offices. There, staff people can offer constituents brochures, pocket Constitutions, maps, warm words, and a lasting impression of the diligence and concern of their lawmakers.

Visits to the Capitol have dropped like a rock since September 11. To pick one indicator, the kiosk of the U.S. Capitol Historical Society, in the middle of the Capitol, averaged 17,000 visitors per day before the attacks; since, the kiosk has received about 300 per day. Paranoia about anthrax all over Congress obviously hasn't helped, but the additional security measures taken since the attacks have also made a difference. Never a particularly visitor-friendly place, the Capitol was at least open and accessible. Now, surrounded by security personnel and concrete barriers, the open house of the people seems more like an armed camp. It is extremely difficult to get into—or exit—the Capitol, with concrete barriers, metal detectors, Capitol police, and National Guard troops everywhere. In October, Congress reinforced these physical barriers with a procedural one, postponing tours of the Capitol itself for nearly two months.

Finally, there's the matter of travel. Since the arrival of jet airplanes, most members of Congress have gone home every weekend—spending their time giving speeches, holding office hours for constituents, and glad-handing at nursing homes and schools. (Indeed, most newly elected members now keep their families in their districts rather than moving them to Washington.) As such, lawmakers have honed to precision a certain schedule. Working on Capitol Hill from Tuesday to Thursday, members of Congress typically stay late at the Capitol on Thursdays and then race to nearby Reagan National Airport—where they enjoy special privileges like close-in parking—to catch the last flights out of town, often with seconds to spare.

But lately this precise schedule has gotten all mucked up. Reagan National, of course, closed down entirely for weeks following the attacks, then reopened with sharply curtailed flight schedules and new, heavy security procedures. Many members once used to the convenience of an eight- to ten-minute drive to Reagan National now have to look elsewhere—Dulles International Airport, which is 40 minutes from Capitol Hill, or Baltimore-Washington International Airport, which is more than an hour away.

Unfortunately, none of these disruptions are likely to be short-term. Even after the current mail backlog is cleared, new security measures will have to be employed, sharply slowing down delivery and increasing constituent crankiness. Similarly, even assuming there are no further anthrax scares or other terrorist incidents, it's doubtful that the number of visitors to Capitol Hill will return to its pre-September 11 level any time soon. And the lawmakers themselves, faced with the new realities of air travel, will likely wind up going home less often or shortening the amount of time they spend there when they do. Several Republican House members have already talked to Majority Leader Dick Armey about changing the House floor schedule to make it more family-friendly.

With jet air travel and modern telecommunications, Congress grew almost obsessively close to constituents in recent decades, in some cases subordinating thoughtful deliberation to real-time, campaign-style interactions with voters. But those connections—including the opportunity for average voters to see their lawmakers up close and personal, and to know that they have direct access—are a cornerstone of America's form of democracy, one of the characteristics that distinguishes Congress from most parliaments. A Capitol that resembles an armed camp, and a growing sense of physical remove between our representatives and those they represent, is a sore price to pay in the nation's war on terrorism. But for the time being, it's not clear we have a choice.

Michael C. Dorf

The Supreme Court Returns, to a Changed Legal Landscape

The Supreme Court returned to work this week with a range of familiar hot-button issues on its docket: affirmative action, capital punishment, and school vouchers, among others. The cases the Court will

Michael C. Dorf is Vice Dean and Professor of Law at Columbia University School of Law.

decide over the next nine months are no doubt important to the litigants and the people whose lives they will affect. Yet in the aftermath of September 11, the divisions among the Justices must be seen in a different perspective.

For the last two decades we have been told that America is fighting a culture "war," with the Supreme Court a "battlefield," and the Justices themselves sometime "combatants." Now we know better. These metaphors are entirely wrong—not just because after September 11, they seem to trivialize war, but also because the Justices were never truly at war with each other, but rather in heated debate. And debate is not a type of war, or a step away from war; it is the opposite of war.

A Divided Court with a Shared Commitment

Whether the Constitution requires, permits, or prohibits abortion, affirmative action, the death penalty, or school vouchers are questions that we can passionately debate in a variety of fora. But even as we debate them, we recognize that our shared commitment to resolving these questions peacefully—through reasoned discussion, judicial decisions, and political action, not violence—is more fundamental, and ultimately more important, than any particular resolution at which we might arrive.

The terrorists who destroyed the World Trade Center and damaged the Pentagon epitomized what we are against, but they also showed us what we are for. As our leaders all implore us to return to our familiar routines and thereby resist giving in to terrorism, it is appropriate for the Court—and for Court-watchers—to focus on the mundane and not-so-mundane questions that inevitably arise in any functioning democracy. Yet perhaps the new reality will enable the Court to put aside whatever bitter feelings linger from *Bush v. Gore*, and recognize that principled (or even unprincipled) disagreement is no cause for division.

Issues on the Horizon

In a speech given last week in New York, Justice Sandra Day O'Connor stated that government efforts to combat terrorism on the home front will raise "tough questions" that will "require a great deal of study, goodwill and expertise to resolve them." What she did not state, but what is obvious nonetheless, is that the final responsibility for resolving many of these tough questions will rest with her Court.

It is still too soon to know exactly which of the proposed changes in law enforcement and counter-terrorism strategy will become official policy. Nonetheless, it is already clear that three sorts of issues are likely to arise: questions of equality, of privacy, and of due process.

Equality Issues for Arab-Americans and Muslim-Americans

Virtually all responsible political leaders have condemned stereotyping of Arab-Americans and Muslim-Americans. As a result, wholesale official discrimination of the sort our government perpetrated against Japanese-Americans during World War II—and that the Court failed to condemn in its egregious decision in *Korematsu v. United States*—is not a realistic possibility.

Still, some attention to national origin and religion may play *a role* in proactive measures by law enforcement. Suppose the FBI monitors chat rooms on Arab language websites to a much greater degree than it monitors other websites (such as, for example, the *Writ* Message Boards). Because chat rooms are public, there would be no privacy violation—but there would be an equality question.

Singling people out for surveillance on the basis of language or nationality would pose a prima facie equality issue—even if the surveillance does not implicate Fourth Amendment limits on warrantless searches and seizures.

Under standard constitutional doctrine, government actions taken on the basis of race, ethnicity, or religion typically lead to exacting judicial scrutiny. But the constitutional provisions implicated would be the Fifth and Fourteenth Amendments, with their guarantee of equal protection of the law, not the Fourth Amendment.

Privacy and Balancing

Lawyers and judges who are uncomfortable about ethnic profiling—even if ethnicity is only one piece of the profile—may favor law enforcement techniques that subject *everyone* to greater surveillance. Indeed, some civil libertarians have already argued that this is the appropriate line.

Subjecting only a small subset of the population to far-reaching law enforcement techniques risks going too far, some say. But if those techniques affect everyone equally, the public will cry foul when the line has been crossed, and too much privacy has been sacrificed for security.

For example, the public likely would not tolerate strip-searches of all airline passengers—but it might tolerate such searches if applied, for example, only to those passengers who fit an ethnic profile. If the choice is between strip-searches for all, and strip-searches for none, the public may choose more carefully.

Notice how this argument pits the privacy of all against equality—or more precisely, against the privacy of some. To protect the constitutional value of equality may, in other words, require some sacrifice of the constitutional value of privacy. Put another way, according to this argument, a greater number of people may have to endure searches that, to some extent, limit their privacy, so that an ethnic minority does not have to endure even more invasive searches.

The tradeoff I have described has always been implicit in the law, but it now may become explicit. Jurists like Justice Antonin Scalia have long criticized balancing tests as providing judges with too much discretion. Such judges prefer "bright-line rules." Yet as future cases increasingly present constitutional rights and values on each side of the scales, balancing may become unavoidable.

When the Fourth Amendment is pitted against the Fifth or Fourteenth Amendment, and privacy against equal protection, there will be no easy answers.

So too, we can expect the government to argue—not without good reason—that security itself is a constitutional value. Liberals who have long contended that the meaning of constitutional language like "unreasonable searches and seizures" should be interpreted flexibly to bar some police practices that were permitted in the Eighteenth Century, should now expect that argument to be turned in the opposite direction. A law enforcement technique that may be unreasonable if used against a petty thief, it will be argued, is entirely reasonable if employed against a terrorist.

Due Process Questions

Although President Bush and others declared the September 11 attack an act of war, the United States has, until recently, treated terrorism as a species of crime. The government indicted and prosecuted the people who attempted to destroy the World Trade Center in 1993 and even before the latest events, Osama Bin Laden was under indictment for his role in the bombing of U.S. embassies in Kenya and Tanzania.

Already a debate has begun over whether to treat the terrorism threat as a military or a criminal matter—or more properly, over what mix of military and law enforcement techniques to deploy.

Of course, at this point, it would be foolish to impose a criminal justice template on every aspect of operations. Due process norms—such as the accused's right to notice of the charges against him, his right to confront the witnesses against him, or the right to an attorney—can hardly be applied on the battlefield.

Yet at the same time, some substantial portion of the government response will use domestic legal processes, in which citizens, aliens, and their lawyers will undoubtedly press conventional legal claims. These claims are likely to pull the Justices in two competing directions.

A Court Torn Between Two Doctrines

On the one hand, there is a long tradition of judicial deference to executive authority in wartime. Accordingly, to the extent that the Justices perceive the domestic legal response as a piece of the larger strategy, they will likely sustain at least those measures—such as closed trials and perhaps even secret evidence—for which the government can offer a plausible national security rationale.

On the other hand, in recent years the current Supreme Court has taken a remarkably expansive view of its power, conceiving the federal judiciary as not merely one branch of government, but as the pre-eminent one. This view may come into conflict with the tradition of deference to the executive in national security matters.

The most obvious example of the Court's view of itself as first among equals is *Bush v. Gore*. There, the Court ignored the claim that Congress was the appropriate body to resolve the election dispute. But the attitude that the Court has the first and last word is shared by *all* the Justices—not just those in the *Bush v. Gore* majority.

Consider two immigration cases decided in June, *INS v. St. Cyr* and *Zadvydas v. Davis*. In both cases, the majority included the four *Bush v. Gore* dissenters. (They were joined, respectively, by Justice Kennedy in *St. Cyr* and Justice O'Connor in *Zadvydas*.) Both decisions went to great lengths to find that Congress had not eliminated the availability of a writ of habeas corpus to aliens. In so doing, they both affirmed a substantial judicial role even in immigration matters—traditionally a subject over which Congress has considerable discretion (and one that arguably has an inherent relationship to national security).

In *St. Cyr*, the Court allowed a challenge to deportation of an alien; in *Zadvydas* the Court allowed a challenge to indefinite detention of an alien. These decisions will no doubt be invoked if, in the coming months, the government seeks to detain terrorism suspects without trial—or, conceivably, deport aliens who are associated with terrorists but not accused of crimes.

Only time will tell whether a Supreme Court that has lately preferred its own power to that of the other branches of government will revert to the historical practice of judicial deference to executive and legislative authority that customarily occurs during wartime.

The Politics of Organized Interests

David E. Rosenbaum

Since Sept. 11, Lobbyists Use New Pitches for Old Pleas

The war against terrorism has created some novel pitches from Washington lobbyists, now swarming over the capital as Congress tries to wrap up its business for the year.

The American Traffic Safety Services Association, whose members make traffic signs, is arguing that more federal money is needed for road signs to prevent traffic jams after terror attacks. California date growers have petitioned the White House and the Pentagon to buy dates for food packages being dropped in Afghanistan. They would be a treat for the Afghans during Ramadan, the growers maintain.

What happened was a tragedy, certainly, but there are opportunities. We're in business. This is not a charity.

James Albertin Corporate Lobbyist

Since Sept. 11, many other business lobbyists have taken old pleas for federal help and turned them into new arguments for spending to combat terrorism. Representative Edward J. Markey, Democrat of Massachusetts, is amused by the efforts to profit from patriotism.

"No self-respecting lobbyist," he said, has not "repackaged his position as a patriotic response to the tragedy."

This, he said, is what he is hearing:

"The challenge is terrorism. The answer is re-establish telecommunications monopolies."

"The challenge is terrorism. The answer is to drill for oil in the Arctic Wildlife Refuge."

"The challenge is terrorism. The answer is a $15 billion retroactive tax break to scores of corporations."

The minute he arrived at work on the morning of Sept. 12, a top aide to a Democratic senator recalled, he received a call from a lobbyist for the airline industry pushing for a repeal of the federal tax on jet fuel to help the industry in the aftermath of the terrorist attacks.

Over the next few days, the aide said, reading from his desk calendar and telephone logs, he heard from representatives of the travel, insurance, telecommunications and software industries, from lobbyists for farmers, pharmaceutical companies and manufacturers, and from several military contractors.

None of them asked for anything different from what they had sought from Congress before, the aide said, but all had new pitches presenting their cases as responses to the attacks.

Until Sept. 11, money was scarce. President Bush and Congress had said they would save the surplus in the Social Security accounts. But now, fiscal discipline has been played down, budget deficits are the order of the day and companies, unions and the range of interest groups want a slice of a vast new stimulus-military- bioterrorism-homeland defense pie.

The idea of making money from the attacks sounds so crass that few lobbyists are willing to talk about it openly. But James Albertine, a lobbyist who represents companies, trade associations and nonprofit organizations, was remarkably frank. "What happened was a tragedy, certainly, but there are opportunities," Mr. Albertine said. "We're in business. This is not a charity."

Paul C. Light, director of government studies at the Brookings Institution, put it directly. "This is the best of times for lobbyists," Mr.

Light said. "All of a sudden, they are in a position where they can sell their clients on the possibility of success."

Some of the lobbyists have such clear cases that their clients were damaged by the terrorism and need immediate relief that the government has already come through or seems very likely to. The $15 billion package of aid and loan guarantees for the airline industry, enacted in September, is an example, although some critics have assailed its size.

Insurance companies, which were busily lobbying in the House last week, can expect some form of federal protection against large losses from future terrorist attacks, although it remains unclear what form the aid will take. New York City has a strong claim for federal assistance to rebuild the devastated area, though the amount of money that will be available is a matter of considerable dispute.

As for economic stimulus, the Republican package the House of Representatives approved in October was made up principally of corporate tax breaks: larger write-offs for investments in plants and equipment, retroactive repeal of the alternative minimum tax, tax savings for financial services companies with operations abroad and a lower capital gains tax.

Michael Baroody, chief lobbyist for the National Association of Manufacturers, made this argument for how cutting corporate taxes would help revive the economy: "Companies are either going to invest the extra money in equipment, or they're going to invest it in jobs."

But even Mr. Baroody, who put together a coalition of corporate lobbyists to press for prospective repeal of the minimum tax—a measure enacted in 1986 to make sure profitable companies could not escape income taxes—did not defend the House plan for repealing it retroactively.

That plan, denounced by Democrats, would result in hundreds of millions of dollars in tax refunds to corporations, including International Business Machines, General Motorsand General Electric.

Here are some other commercial interests that have adjusted their pitches in response to the attacks:

- The travel industry is seeking a temporary $1,000 tax credit per family to help offset vacation expenses.
- Boeing , with the Marine Corps, is pressing Congress and the Pentagon to revive the V-22 Osprey, an experimental aircraft that has been grounded because of fatal crashes.
- Verizon Communications wants to lift federal rules that give smaller competitors access to its network. The company argues

that its success in restoring telephone service to Lower Manhattan demonstrates the importance to the nation of large telecommunications companies.

- Farm lobbyists are portraying a subsidy bill as a safety net for farmers in the recession and a bulwark against disruptions in food supplies in war time. Once called the Agriculture Act of 2001, it has been renamed the Farm Security Act of 2001.

Many, maybe most, of these proposals will never become law or public policy. But that is not so important to lobbyists, said Charles Peters, the founding editor of The Washington Monthly magazine and a cryptographer of the codes of Washington. "I can hear them saying, 'Oh, God, we fought hard on this amendment,'" Mr. Peters said. "'We got it through the House. That's worth another $2 million in billing.'"

When the Senate took up a bill to extend the moratorium on sales taxes on purchases over the Internet, both sides tried to take advantage of how times had changed. Those who wanted to end the moratorium said states needed the sales tax revenue because of their new expenses for homeland security. And those who wanted to continue the moratorium said taxes would further depress sales that have dropped since Sept. 11.

Barry Yeoman and Bill Hogan

Airline Insecurity

Federal regulators have known for years that the nation's system of airport security was "seriously flawed." But the FAA repeatedly placed politics and profits above the public's safety.

The buzzer sounded at an awkward moment for Rep. Don Young. The Alaska Republican was halfway through a press conference on October 17, explaining why he was trying to derail efforts to turn over the screening of airline passengers to federal law enforcement officers. Six days earlier, the Senate had unanimously passed a bill that would overhaul the way airports staff their metal detectors and X-ray checkpoints. Rather than relying on private security companies, whose minimum-wage workers routinely fail to detect guns and bombs, the bill called for hiring 28,000 better-paid and better-trained government agents. But Young considered this a "knee-jerk" reaction to the September 11 terrorist attacks. "My wife Lu flies quite a lot, as do my two daughters," he told reporters. "I want my family and all Americans to have the best air security possible." Still, he added, he did not want "to tie the president's hands and force him to hire only federal employees."

As Young started to field questions, a mechanical screech alerted House members that they were needed across the street at the Capitol for a vote. The congressman huddled with his fellow Republicans behind the podium. "We'll be back," he said—with that, he handed over the microphone to a man named Kenneth Quinn, who wasted no time blasting the Senate bill. "A nationalized approach to security is a step backward in the war against terrorism," Quinn declared. Rather than relying on "civil servants," he said, the government should "inspire the private sector's competitive juices."

Quinn was no congressional aide filling in for absent lawmakers. He works for the Aviation Security Association, a lobbying group for private screening companies. His clients, who are paid $700 million by the airlines each year to screen passengers and baggage, have been cited repeatedly for sloppy performance. Many pay their employees so little—wages are sometimes $11,000 a year, with few benefits—workers must hold down two jobs to make ends meet. Almost all wind up quitting: On average, airports are forced to replace their entire screening workforces every year. In October 2000, a federal judge ordered the largest company, Argenbright Security, to pay a fine of $1 million for hiring violent felons, falsifying their background checks, and "training" the new hires with 45-minute videos. As reporters took notes at the press conference, however, Quinn declared that taking business away from companies like Argenbright would be "a huge mistake."

A month later, Congress voted to replace private screeners with federal employees. But Young's decision to leave a corporate lobbyist running the show underscores why airports have remained unsafe for so long. A review by Mother Jones of court documents, lobbying disclosure forms, campaign finance records, government audits, and the docket of the Federal Aviation Administration—well as interviews with numerous experts—that when it comes to airline security, the aviation industry has remained firmly in control. With the cooperation of the FAA, industry leaders have scuttled or watered down just about every significant reform that has been proposed over the past dozen years, including the recommendations of two high-profile presidential commissions.

They've accomplished this, in part, through generous campaign contributions: The airlines gave almost $4.2 million to both political parties during the 2000 elections. They've also deployed a squadron of lobbyists that includes the best—best-connected—that money can buy. More than half of the airline industry's 200 lobbyists used to work on Capitol Hill or in the executive branch, including 10 former members of Congress, 2 former transportation secretaries, 3 former high-ranking FAA officials, and 15 former White House aides. Quinn was the FAA's top lawyer under the elder President Bush. Linda Hall Daschle, the wife of Senate Majority Leader Tom Daschle, worked for the Air Transport Association, a lobbying group composed of the major airlines, before serving as the FAA's acting administrator under President Clinton; she now lobbies for American and Northwest airlines. All told, the top nine U.S. airlines and their lobbying group typically spend more than $15 million a year lobbying Congress, the Department of Transportation, the FAA, the National Transportation Safety Board, and the White House.

"Clearly, from my experience, the airline industry has one of the most formidable and most aggressive groups of lobbyists representing any industry," says Senator Peter Fitzgerald, a Republican from Illinois. "In the three years that I've been in Washington, I don't think I've seen anything the airlines favor die, or anything they oppose pass."

Since September 11, Americans have become all too familiar with the flaws in the nation's aviation security. Throughout the 1990s, government inspections designed to intentionally breach airport security met with extraordinary success. Federal inspectors found they could smuggle firearms, hand grenades, and bomb components past screening checkpoints at every airport they visited. They could walk onto planes and place objects in the cabins. They could get into cargo holds. In one probe conducted in 1999, they successfully boarded 117 airplanes—filled with passengers—were asked to show identification only one-fourth of the time. Mary Schiavo, the inspector general for the Department of Transportation from 1990 to 1996, says her office repeatedly recommended security improvements, including a system to match checked bags with onboard passengers. "The FAA simply didn't want to hear about it," she says. "They said since we had never had a major domestic terrorist incident against aviation, the risk was low."

Ever since 1988, when a bomb in a suitcase destroyed Pan Am Flight 103 over Lockerbie, Scotland, experts have sounded increasingly forceful alarms. "The U.S. civil aviation security system is seriously flawed and has failed to provide the proper level of protection for the traveling public," concluded a 1990 report by the President's

Commission on Aviation Security and Terrorism, appointed by then-President Bush. "This system needs major reform.

The Bush commission's report recommended dozens of new measures. It called for more rigorous training of the workers who screen passengers entering airport terminals. It proposed a system to ensure that a would-be bomber doesn't check a suitcase full of explosives onto a plane and then fail to board himself. And, upon learning that some of the baggage clerks working for Flight 103 had criminal records, the commission recommended the FBI run background checks on everyone working at airports. "The case for mandatory criminal-record checks for airport employees is at least as compelling as for employees in industries such as securities and banking," the panel concluded.

But the airline industry used its clout to block implementation of the new criminal-check rule. The Air Transport Association argued the measure would cost the airlines more than $1 billion, with limited effectiveness. To press its case, it hired a man who could normally be expected to advocate background checks: William Webster, the former director of the FBI and CIA. Webster argued the reform "would subject the industry to a very heavy diversion of resources" without catching would-be bombers. The lobbying worked: It took the FAA five years to adopt a rule to weed out criminals—in the end, it required the industry to conduct background checks only on employees with access to secure areas who had long gaps in their employment histories.

Few regulatory agencies give industry lobbyists as warm a welcome as the FAA. For its first 38 years, the close relationship was codified into the law: The agency's twofold mission was to safeguard the traveling public and to promote the aviation industry. Although Congress eliminated the FAA's promotional role in 1996, airline executives and lobbyists continue to enjoy "direct and frequent access to the administration," says Gerald Dillingham, director of civil aviation issues for the General Accounting Office, the investigative arm of Congress. "Not only do they lobby the administration, but oftentimes they serve on advisory panels the agency puts together." The agency frequently holds "industry days," in which airline executives are briefed on hot issues and given an opportunity to make recommendations behind closed doors. The calendars of FAA officials are filled with appointments with lobbyists, and many of the agency's senior employees wind up leaving to work for the private sector. Besides Quinn and Linda Daschle, former FAA Chief Counsel E. Tazwell Ellet now lobbies for the Air Transport Association, and former Assistant Chief Counsel Albert Randall works for American and Northwest.

As a result, many officials acknowledge, the agency has come to perceive issues the same way industry does. The process begins as soon as FAA administrators are nominated. "In order to get confirmed, they have to go around kissing the rings of the powers-that-be in the industry," says Jim Burnett, who chaired the National Transportation Safety Board under President Reagan. "It's a process of visiting with people who have power and trying to reassure them that you will not be a threat."

By 1995, when the FAA finally passed its rule requiring limited background checks, a leading congressional expert on airline security was growing concerned about how little progress had been made since the Lockerbie crash. That May, Rep. Jim Oberstar, a Minnesota Democrat, wrote to President Clinton, urging him to convene a blue-ribbon panel to review the system from top to bottom. For a year, nothing happened. It took another air disaster to trigger the next flurry of high-level discussions.

Just before the 1996 Olympics, TWA Flight 800 went down off the coast of Long Island in what was initially believed to be a bombing or missile attack. The explosion had eerie resonances for Victoria Cummock, who had lost her husband over Lockerbie. The Miami widow, who had become an advocate for air crash victims, flew to New York to meet the families of TWA passengers. In a hangar at Kennedy Airport, she met with President Clinton, who invited her to serve on the brand-new White House Commission on Aviation Safety and Security. The commission would be chaired by Vice President Al Gore, lending it considerable credibility and power. It would include scientists, military experts, and high-ranking government officials. "My heart sang," Cummock says, recalling her conversation with the president. "I thought, 'Oh my God, thank God.'"

Her enthusiasm was short-lived. The Gore commission, as it was known, became one of the clearest examples of how politics and profit have eclipsed public safety. At their very first meeting, the commissioners were surprised to receive a pre-written set of recommendations prepared by staff members. "We were just going to rubber-stamp them," Cummock recalls. "With each recommendation, I remember saying, 'With all due respect, Mr. Vice President, do you realize that...?' People were horrified that I was interrupting the flow. They kept telling me, 'Ms. Cummock, the vice president has a press conference, then he needs to get on to other meetings.'"

Cummock didn't know it at the time, but the commission's initial report was a done deal before she ever saw it. A CIA memo written the day before the meeting indicates that the agency was working with the staff behind the scenes to ensure that the panel offered no dissent to the preapproved proposals. "The government members of the commission are lined up to support the recommendations," Richard Haver, a CIA official assigned to assist the committee, reported to his agency's director. Cummock, though, was a different matter. "She is a very intelligent, intense, and attractive individual," he wrote, noting that he had tried "schmoozing" her several weeks earlier. "My estimate is that she can be kept in line if she believes progress is going to result from the effort. If she believes the effort is headed in the direction of appeasing the airlines, whom she distrusts, then she could become a major problem."

Immediately after the first meeting, Gore and his aides held press conferences to highlight the panel's "common-sense solutions." One of the proposals, which Cummock endorsed, was called "full bag match." Every piece of luggage loaded onto an airplane would have to be matched to a passenger on board. Any unmatched suitcase, like the one containing the bomb that killed Cummock's husband, would have to be removed before takeoff. The airlines claimed that matching bags would be time-consuming and expensive, but a study by the University of California, partly funded by the FAA, found that full bag match would take barely one minute per flight. "You probably won't even notice it," said Elaine Kamarck, one of Gore's top political advisers, at a press briefing held on September 11, 1996.

The airlines noticed. "We were vigorously opposed to it," says Dick Doubrava, managing director of security for the Air Transport Association. Insisting that the delays from bag matching would "impact the whole integrity of the system," the association and its member airlines launched a full-bore lobbying campaign. They met with the commission staff. They made the rounds on Capitol Hill. They leaned on members of Congress, who in turn pressured the commission to back off. And although Kamarck insists that "the vice president never met with the industry," officials at the Air Transport Association recall otherwise, noting that their president, Carol Hallett, had plenty of access to the White House. "She would routinely see Gore all the time," Doubrava says.

Eight days after Kamarck's press briefing, Gore sent a letter to Hallett backing off on his call for an immediate move toward full bag match. "I want to make it very clear that it is not the intent of this administration or of the commission to create a hardship for the air transportation industry or to cause inconvenience to the traveling public," he wrote. Instead of sticking with the original plan to match all bags to passengers, Gore began calling for an industry-backed alternative, in which a computerized profiling system would monitor suspicious travelers and remove their bags if they failed to board planes. The new plan was blasted by security experts, who concluded it would be simple for terrorists to evade the profiling system.

The nation's airlines wasted no time in expressing their thanks. The day after Gore's letter, TWA sent $40,000 to the Democratic National Committee, which was headed into the final weeks of the 1996 campaign. A month later, American Airlines came through with three contributions of $83,333 made over five days—$250,000 burst of beneficence that it has never again matched. In the last days of the push to re-elect Clinton and Gore, Democratic Party committees also raked in $83,000 from Northwest Airlines, $117,465 from United Airlines, and $15,000 from US Airways. In all, the major airlines poured more than $500,000 into various Democratic soft-money accounts in the weeks following Gore's letter—and a half times what they gave Republicans during the same period.

Michael Wascom, vice president of the Air Transport Association, calls the contributions "strictly coincidental." Kamarck, the Gore political adviser, says the prospect of campaign donations had no influence on Gore's decision to write the letter. "It didn't make a f— difference," she says. "It was October of an election year. We were 15 points ahead of Bob Dole. Everyone was giving money." In fact, the commission's staff seemed as intent on raising money as it was on improving airline safety. According to documents obtained by Mother Jones, campaign aides on the staff used the commission's offices, fax machine, and letterhead to draft a speech for the Democratic National Convention and to assist Maria Hsia, the party operative later convicted in the Buddhist temple fundraising scandal. When industry executives were asked to assist the commission, the requests often came from staffers who were assisting the campaign.

As the commission kept meeting in preparation for the release of its final report, the industry continued to lean on commissioners. A few months after the election, Billie Vincent, former director of civilian aviation security for the FAA, spoke with commission member Brian Jenkins, an antiterrorism consultant whose clients included the airlines. "He was distraught," recalls Vincent. "He related to me that somebody from the airline industry—wouldn't say who—contacted him and told him they were angry with his positions. They told him he should remember how much business the airlines were giving him."

In public hearings, commissioners sat quietly through testimony by various experts, rarely asking tough questions. In the final months, they grew even less interested in security issues after the crash of TWA

Flight 800 was traced to faulty wiring rather than an act of terrorism. The FBI and CIA continued to warn the commission that serious holes remained in the security system, and Cummock urged her colleagues not to back off. When she pressed for more meaningful give-and-take on security issues, a commission staff member pulled her aside and told her that the Christmas decorations had been put up at the White House. "If you'd like," she recalls the aide telling her, "we could arrange a VIP tour."

When the Gore commission issued its final report in February 1997, the industry was pleased. The commission called for a slow approach to bag match, calling it a "contentious and difficult area." It suggested private security companies be certified by the government, but made no mention of improving wages or benefits. And it gave the FAA two more years to implement FBI fingerprint checks on airport workers. The Air Transport Association praised the document as a "good compendium of the issues that the industry and the FAA and the government at large have been looking at for some time."

Armed with the report, the FAA vowed to develop rules to accomplish the broad mandates outlined by the commission. Over the next four years, however, the airlines mounted an all-out campaign to forestall or weaken the already-diluted security proposals. The industry filed myriad objections to the rules, asking for delays and calling for public hearings. "The rule-making process is very easily manipulated by someone with a lot of money and expertise, and the airlines have that in spades," says Rep. Peter DeFazio, an Oregon Democrat. "Anything that would cost them money they could fight, and delay rule making for years and years." According to Elaine Kamarck, federal regulators didn't bother to fight back. "The FAA decided to pick its battles with the airlines," she says. "You had a sluggish bureaucracy under pressure from the corporate world. They paid lip service, but let the rules drag on."

Paul Takemoto, a spokesman for the FAA, insists the agency took the rules seriously but needed input from the airlines. "We move as fast as we can, with the understanding that we need to make sure that we're doing it right," he says. But according to a study by the General Accounting Office, it sometimes takes the agency 5 years or more to begin the rule-making process—up to 15 years to complete it. All that while, says DeFazio, "the Air Transport Association, with its huge staff and budget, is working day in and day out to prevent things from happening."

The FAA did suggest criminal-background checks on more airport employees with gaps in their employment records, including workers who screen passengers, baggage, and cargo. But the airlines claimed that vetting their current workers would be an administrative headache. "They have been good employees and do not pose a threat to aviation," TWA argued in a letter to the FAA in May 1997. "This proposed requirement would not do anything to increase aviation security. It would only add unnecessary costs and paperwork to the industry." The same day, a lobbying group for airport-service companies called the National Air Transportation Association weighed in, protesting that it would be difficult to run checks on baggage and cargo screeners, fuel truck operators, and other workers whose previous employers often kept few records.

In the end, the FAA narrowed its rule even further. It exempted baggage and cargo screeners from background checks, and called for checks only on new applicants for passenger-screening jobs with long employment gaps—than 1 percent of all airport workers hired. Federal agents are now investigating the possibility that the September 11 hijackers were aided by renegade airport employees.

While the FAA did issue a modest rule on criminal checks, it issued no rule at all on another key recommendation of the Gore plan. The commission had recommended that before an airline hires a private security firm to screen passengers and baggage, the federal government must certify that the company provides minimal training for workers and periodically tests their performance. Congress ordered the FAA to create a certification rule by May 2001.

The Air Transport Association insists it has always supported screening-company certification. "There was no resistance," says Doubrava, the group's security chief. But a review of government dockets shows that the airlines themselves were quietly working to delay and weaken the regulation that the FAA eventually came up with. "The proposed rule will have a major economic impact on Alaska Airlines' long-term conducting of business," a company executive wrote to the FAA in April 2000. The letter enumerated three pages of specific objections, arguing that it would "not be cost-effective" to recertify companies every five years and adding that the airline didn't want to be held responsible if one of its screening companies violated the law. The next day, Midway Airlines chimed in, calling it an "unnecessary burden" to require that employees have a week of full-time experience before training newcomers. And United Express said it supported screener certification—long as the FAA exempted all existing security firms from the "rigorous application process." In the end, the FAA missed its congressional deadline, and the rule plodded its way through the bureaucratic process without being approved.

In the first weeks after the September 11 attacks, measures that had previously been stalled were suddenly put on the fast track. FAA administrator Jane Garvey ordered criminal-history checks for all airport workers with access to secure areas. She also ordered the acceleration of a program to put in new machines to detect explosives at the nation's largest airports. "Everything has changed," says Takemoto, the FAA spokesman. "It's a completely different environment. It should make it easier to accomplish things that, sadly, we would not have been able to accomplish before September 11."

Those emergency measures, though, didn't solve the underlying problems. A month after the hijackings, a passenger made it through the security checkpoint in New Orleans International Airport and onto a Southwest flight carrying a loaded derringer. Two weeks later, workers employed by Argenbright Security failed to detain a man who passed through a checkpoint at Chicago's O'Hare International Airport with a stun gun, a can of pepper spray, and nine knives.

Nevertheless, industry officials continued to fight measures to help prevent airline terrorism, citing their concerns for the bottom line. At one recent congressional hearing, Alaska Airlines president John Kelly spoke out against a $2.50 to $3 surcharge to pay for enhanced security, suggesting the fee would scare away potential passengers. "The people do not respond to anything other than the total price," he told the House Transportation Committee. "That is strictly supply and demand." When Rep. DeFazio suggested that airline tickets could say "security surcharge" in large letters, Kelly remained unmoved. "People still make decisions on whether to fly based on how much it costs," he said.

Private security companies also fought efforts to place airport screening in the hands of federal law enforcement officers. "No one would think of contracting out the FBI," said Senator Fritz Hollings, a South Carolina Democrat, during a debate in October over the Senate bill to federalize the screening workforce. "No one would ever think about contracting out the security and protection of the president." But despite the unanimous vote in the Senate to eliminate private contractors, Republicans in the House sided with the security firms, passing an alternative bill on November 1 that would have kept the screening business in the hands of private companies unless the president ordered otherwise. Bush backed the measure, and the airlines bowed out of the fight, saying only that they no longer wanted responsibility for overseeing screeners.

On November 16, lawmakers finally agreed on a compromise to make all airport screeners federal employees. But in a nod to private screening companies, airports will be given what Rep. Don Young calls the "flexibility" to opt out of the system after three years and resume contracting with private firms.

Even with the increase in federal oversight, security experts note that it will take more than a single law to make air travel truly secure. Jim Burnett, the former head of the National Transportation Safety Board, says that unless federal regulators take a tougher approach — that doesn't place the industry's profit margins above all else — reforms will continue to drag on for years, stalled by industry lobbying and regulatory inaction. "If the FAA doesn't move away from the consensus-type regulatory behavior," he says, "we may walk away from these things with a lot of visible steps being taken, but without really having put in an effective security system."

Terrorist Challenges to an Open Society

Internal Security Confronts Civil Liberties

....

Richard A. Posner

Security Versus Civil Liberties

A distinguished jurist advises us to calm down about the probable curtailing of some personal freedoms in the months ahead. As a nation we've treated certain civil liberties as malleable, when necessary, from the start

In the wake of the September 11 terrorist attacks have come many proposals for tightening security; some measures to that end have already been taken. Civil libertarians are troubled. They fear that concerns about national security will lead to an erosion of civil liberties.

They offer historical examples of supposed overreactions to threats to national security. They treat our existing civil liberties—freedom of the press, protections of privacy and of the rights of criminal suspects, and the rest—as sacrosanct, insisting that the battle against international terrorism accommodate itself to them.

I consider this a profoundly mistaken approach to the question of balancing liberty and security. The basic mistake is the prioritizing of liberty. It is a mistake about law and a mistake about history. Let me begin with law. What we take to be our civil liberties—for example, immunity from arrest except upon probable cause to believe we've committed a crime, and from prosecution for violating a criminal statute enacted after we committed the act that violates it—were made legal rights by the Constitution and other enactments. The other enactments can be changed relatively easily, by amendatory legislation. Amending the Constitution is much more difficult. In recognition of this the Framers left most of the constitutional provisions that confer rights pretty vague. The courts have made them definite.

Concretely, the scope of these rights has been determined, through an interaction of constitutional text and subsequent judicial interpretation, by a weighing of competing interests. I'll call them the public-safety interest and the liberty interest. Neither, in my view, has priority. They are both important, and their relative importance changes from time to time and from situation to situation. The safer the nation feels, the more weight judges will be willing to give to the liberty interest. The greater the threat that an activity poses to the nation's safety, the stronger will the grounds seem for seeking to repress that activity, even at some cost to liberty. This fluid approach is only common sense. Supreme Court Justice Robert Jackson gave it vivid expression many years ago when he said, in dissenting from a free-speech decision he thought doctrinaire, that the Bill of Rights should not be made into a suicide pact. It was not intended to be such, and the present contours of the rights that it confers, having been shaped far more by judicial interpretation than by the literal text (which doesn't define such critical terms as "due process of law" and "unreasonable" arrests and searches), are alterable in response to changing threats to national security.

If it is true, therefore, as it appears to be at this writing, that the events of September 11 have revealed the United States to be in much greater jeopardy from international terrorism than had previously been believed—have revealed it to be threatened by a diffuse, shadowy enemy that must be fought with police measures as well as military force—it stands to reason that our civil liberties will be curtailed. They *should* be curtailed, to the extent that the benefits in greater security outweigh the costs in reduced liberty. All that can reasonably be asked of the responsible legislative and judicial officials is that they weigh the costs as carefully as the benefits.

It will be argued that the lesson of history is that officials habitually exaggerate dangers to the nation's security. But the lesson of history is the opposite. It is because officials have repeatedly and disastrously underestimated these dangers that our history is as violent as it is. Consider such underestimated dangers as that of secession, which led to the Civil War; of a Japanese attack on the United States, which led to the disaster at Pearl Harbor; of Soviet espionage in the 1940s, which accelerated the Soviet Union's acquisition of nuclear weapons and emboldened Stalin to encourage North Korea's invasion of South Korea; of the installation of Soviet missiles in Cuba, which precipitated the Cuban missile crisis; of political assassinations and outbreaks of urban violence in the 1960s; of the Tet Offensive of 1968; of the Iranian revolution of 1979 and the subsequent taking of American diplomats as hostages; and, for that matter, of the events of September 11.

It is true that when we are surprised and hurt, we tend to overreact—but only with the benefit of hindsight can a reaction be separated into its proper and excess layers. In hindsight we know that interning Japanese-Americans did not shorten World War II. But was this known at the time? If not, shouldn't the Army have erred on the side of caution, as it did? Even today we cannot say with any assurance that Abraham Lincoln was wrong to suspend habeas corpus during the Civil War, as he did on several occasions, even though the Constitution is clear that only Congress can suspend this right. (Another of Lincoln's wartime measures, the Emancipation Proclamation, may also have been unconstitutional.) But Lincoln would have been wrong to cancel the 1864 presidential election, as some urged: by November of 1864 the North was close to victory, and canceling the election would have created a more dangerous precedent than the wartime suspension of habeas corpus. This last example shows that civil liberties remain part of the balance even in the most dangerous of times, and even though their relative weight must then be less.

Lincoln's unconstitutional acts during the Civil War show that even legality must sometimes be sacrificed for other values. We are a nation under law, but first we are a nation. I want to emphasize something else, however: the malleability of law, its pragmatic rather than dogmatic character. The law is not absolute, and the slogan *"Fiat iustitia ruat caelum*" ("Let justice be done though the heavens fall") is dangerous nonsense. The law is a human creation rather than a divine gift, a tool of government rather than a mandarin mystery. It is an instrument for promoting social welfare, and as the conditions essential to that welfare change, so must it change.

Civil libertarians today are missing something else—the opportunity to challenge other public-safety concerns that impair civil liberties. I have particularly in mind the war on drugs. The sale of illegal drugs is a "victimless" crime in the special but important sense that it is a consensual activity. Usually there is no complaining witness, so in order to bring the criminals to justice the police have to rely heavily on paid informants (often highly paid and often highly unsavory), undercover agents, wiretaps and other forms of electronic surveillance, elaborate sting operations, the infiltration of suspect organizations, random searches, the monitoring of airports and highways, the "profiling" of likely suspects on the basis of ethnic or racial identity or national origin, compulsory drug tests, and other intrusive methods that put pressure on civil liberties. The war on drugs has been a big flop; moreover, in light of what September 11 has taught us about the gravity of the terrorist threat to the United States, it becomes hard to take entirely seriously the threat to the nation that drug use is said to pose. Perhaps it is time to redirect law-enforcement resources from the investigation and apprehension of drug dealers to the investigation and apprehension of international terrorists. By doing so we may be able to minimize the net decrease in our civil liberties that the events of September 11 have made inevitable.

Professor Lewis R. Katz

Anti-Terrorism Laws: Too Much of a Good Thing

The September 11 attack on America was a blow to the heart for all of us who cherish freedom. Not only did the terrorists attack the

Lewis R. Katz is John C. Hutchins Professor of Law at Case Western Reserve University School of Law. He welcomes comments on this essay at JURIST@law.pitt.edu.

Pentagon, a military center, they also calculated and carried out attacks to inflict massive civilian casualties on American soil. The attacks forever destroyed America's sense of security that we were invulnerable at home. In retrospect, it was a misplaced sense of security; the 1993 World Trade Center bombing should have alerted us to our vulnerability and to the determination and hatred of those who would do us harm. It is likely that the Islamic fanatics who planned these attacks have other sleepers within the United States preparing for additional suicide missions and new horror.

In the face of expected on-going attacks, our country's leaders needed to consider expanding government powers to thwart the conspirators. Thus the events of September 11, and even more so, the continuing threat after that date, required me to analyze the framework that I had constructed to balance individual rights and government authority, and to re-evaluate some of my long-felt notions of limited government. Most of my career has been spent examining the relationship of the government and the people of the United States as reflected within the framework of the Fourth Amendment. Since 1971, police power has grown and the people's protections under the Fourth Amendment have narrowed as police power grew. Generally, I have lamented the balance struck in favor of greater power for the government in areas such as the so-called war on drugs. That war was being lost, and the principal casualty was the Fourth Amendment rights of Americans.

Notwithstanding the Supreme Court rulings of the past thirty years, the current real threat to America impels us to test the Fourth Amendment further. The Fourth Amendment framework is not a straight jacket, or as Justice Robert Jackson put it best, "the Bill of Rights is not a suicide pact." The Amendment prohibits only unreasonable searches and seizures. What is reasonable varies depending upon the circumstances. Government has far greater leeway to intrude upon Fourth Amendment rights and to bypass the Amendment's preferred procedures during a real emergency. During normal times those powers are more limited.

Consequently, we must understand that the Fourth Amendment seeks to ensure a balance between individual rights and legitimate government law enforcement authority. That balance must satisfy two essential ends: it must protect human freedom while accommodating legitimate law enforcement needs. What is reasonable depends upon the immediate circumstances, and the circumstances of September 11 are overwhelming and likely to require additional adjustment to the

Fourth Amendment balance. When viewed through that lens, certain proposals and government conduct, though by no means all, appear reasonable.

The USA Patriot Act of 2001 is a red-flag type of name guaranteed to raise suspicion: What type of extreme government behavior is Congress trying to hide under that apple-pie name? Yet the essentials of the Act do not trouble me. The increased authority to conduct electronic surveillance of telephone and internet communications strikes me as reasonable, for the concept of reasonableness must be flexible enough to incorporate modern technology. The Act expands government eavesdropping authority to include mobile phones and computer communications which were not available and in wide use at the time the power was last defined. Because the terrorists have access to modern technology, the Fourth Amendment command of reasonableness cannot and will not deprive the government of adequate tools for legitimate law enforcement needs. Moreover, the threat is so dire that the command of reasonableness may require the granting of authority that would not be forthcoming in the fight against ordinary crime.

The present emergency also appears to justify a national identification card. I have always loathed the notion of a national ID. My views were shaped by the misuse totalitarian European governments made of such cards. In ordinary times, I might have continued to oppose a national ID. Now, I am no longer adverse to a national ID as a tool to combat terrorists operating the United States. I advocate that such IDs should be equipped with the most current technology, such as retina recognition, to ensure that the person presenting the ID is the one to whom it was issued. No one can be certain that such IDs would have prevented any of the hijackers from boarding any of the four doomed flights, but it may have prevented access to the planes by one or more of the terrorists who were illegally in the United States or whose presence in the United States may have been by then suspect. In any event our efforts now must be geared towards preventing a repeat of September 11.

My acceptance of a national ID in no way signifies acceptance of a proposition that police or government agents may at any time or under any circumstance demand production of that ID. During the Vietnam war some federal officials and local law enforcement officers thought that they could demand to see a young man's draft card at any time. They were wrong; the Fourth Amendment provides standards for stopping and asking individuals for identification. The same rules apply now and would limit when and under what circumstances government agents may ask to see someone's ID. Airports are appropriate venues for such requests. Indiscriminate and arbitrary stops on the street are not.

The events of September 11 also may call for reconsideration of our ideas about racial profiling. The thought of racial and ethnic profiling is an anathema to me. It remains so in the context of police stopping automobiles on the highway. It is not so, however, at an airport boarding station. Nor do I protest when government officials now keep closer tabs on foreign students or elect to make inquiry of some foreign students and not of others. I had no outrage when the FBI talked to one of my students from the Arab gulf region who is a former jet fighter pilot. They checked his bona fides and then left him alone. I was reassured both that they appeared on his doorstep within 72 hours of the September 11 attacks, and later when they elected to leave him alone after speaking with him.

The detention of more than one thousand Arab aliens in the United States is more troubling but not alarming. The decision to detain these men is not in any way reminiscent of the relocation of all Japanese-Americans from the West Coast following the bombing of Pearl Harbor. We are talking about small numbers as well as a very small percentage of Arab aliens present in the United States. I lament that our government will make mistakes, and that innocent people will be detained. The existence of mistakes will not necessarily make the initial or ongoing detention unreasonable. The Fourth Amendment looks for reasonable cause, not perfect reasoning. Moreover, reports of the release of some of these men and their return to their normal lives is reassuring. However, reports of the conditions of the detention and the limitations placed upon the detainees' lawyers are troubling and offensive.

My approval of the Justice Department's policies and behavior is not unlimited. The history of American freedom is based upon the American people's suspicion of government, reinforced in every generation by our government's uncanny ability to push the envelope too far. Government overreaching reinforces suspicion of government, and even in these times we must not simply accept government claims that certain rights should be curtailed.

The Justice Department's announcement that it will eavesdrop on communications between some suspects and their lawyers when the Attorney General has reasonable suspicion that the suspect may disclose information about on-going or future terrorist activities brought my new-found romance with government to a crashing halt. I do not doubt that unusual circumstances might arise where there is legitimate cause to intercept such communications, even though the very concept of such interceptions will have a chilling effect upon the lawyer-client relationship. I am deeply troubled, however, that the administration would claim such authority for the Attorney General rather than acknowledging the preferred constitutional rule which requires prior judicial authorization for such interceptions. Bypassing the neutral and detached magistrate is not necessary, results in the collection of too much power in the executive branch, and is an unreasonable search under the Fourth Amendment and a violation of the Sixth Amendment right to counsel.

As if the decision to encroach on the lawyer-client relationship were not enough to take the bloom off this rose, the White House cut short our honeymoon when it announced that the administration reserves the right to try suspected terrorists before military commissions, whether those persons are apprehended in the United States or in Afghanistan. The Attorney General claims that people who commit such acts should not receive the rights guaranteed under the Bill of Rights to persons accused of crime. Whatever became of the presumption of innocence? Until these people are lawfully convicted, we have no right to assume their guilt. The government has even reserved until later what rules of evidence will prevail at such trials and what standard of proof will be required for a guilty verdict.

I cannot imagine any circumstance that would justify trying any person apprehended in the United States in front of a military commission, without the Sixth Amendment rights that attach to any defendant in a civilian or military court, when the civilian courts are functioning. There is no legitimate necessity for such drastic action which would bypass the fundamental rights which are the hallmark of American justice. We must not sacrifice our most fundamental principles or we run the risk of losing our freedom even at the same time that we prevail over those who hate us for our very system of freedom.

Adam Cohen

Keeping an Eye on Things

A hot rumor swept through the internet privacy world right after the Sept. 11 terrorist attacks. FBI agents had shown up at EarthLink, the nation's third-largest Internet service provider, and ordered it to install Carnivore, the government's controversial device for spying on private citizens' e-mail. But EarthLink, which has long been outspoken about online privacy, flatly refused. Even in a crisis, it seemed, there were still people committed to defending Americans' basic civil liberties.

A great story, but it never happened. EarthLink did, in fact, once tell the FBI it wouldn't let Carnivore be installed on its network. But that was back in December 1999, when the FBI first introduced it. The FBI promptly hauled EarthLink into court, and the G-men and the ISP worked out a deal. EarthLink could use its own software, instead of Carnivore, to monitor e-mail. But it had to turn over all the data the FBI was entitled to under any subpoenas or court orders.

It's hard to blame privacy advocates for trying to find a profile in courage in the Sept. 11 attacks. In the hours after the World Trade Center collapsed, as Americans grieved for 6,000 lost countrymen and braced for more terror, the balance between freedom and security in the national psyche palpably shifted. The government didn't declare martial law—in a way, it didn't have to. Americans were deciding on their own that individual rights will have to yield more to law enforcement. Air travelers, once grumpy about security screening, were suddenly demanding tougher searches, and more probing questioning of suspicious passengers.

It was inevitable that this new mood would affect privacy online. The Sept. 11 terrorists relied heavily on the Internet. Suspected ringleader Mohammed Atta bought his ticket for one of the doomed World Trade Center flights on Americanairlines.com, and the hijackers appear to have plotted their carnage using Yahoo e-mail. And law enforcement was openly predicting a wave of hacking attacks—part of what investigators were calling an e-jihad. When Attorney General John Ashcroft rushed a sweeping antiterrorism bill to Congress, much of it aimed to help the government spy on Americans' use of the Internet.

ADAM COHEN, a senior writer for Time, wrote about online privacy in our July 2000 issue.

In times like these, the arguments for cutting back on privacy are easy. But important as security is, civil libertarians say the nation may come to regret giving law enforcement too much power to monitor American citizens. "These provisions may seem semi-innocuous taken separately by the government we have at the moment," says John Perry Barlow, cofounder of the Electronic Freedom Foundation. "But it has the possibility of turning into a massive surveillance system, where anything you do online can be used against you by a government that is not as benign."

One big winner in the new national climate will be Carnivore. Named for its ability to get at the "meat" in large quantities of e-mail and instant messaging (and recently renamed DCS1000 because the original name sounded so creepy), Carnivore was spawned in the FBI's own labs. And just what is it? The FBI is close-lipped, and ISPs that install it are generally under court order to keep quiet, but it's reported to be a stealthy-looking black box containing a Pentium III with Windows NT, equipped with packet-sniffing software. When the FBI has a suspect whose e-mail it wants to poke through, it gets a court order similar to one for a phone wiretap, takes a Carnivore out of storage in its Quantico, Va., headquarters and works with an ISP's engineers to hook it up to the network.

Once it's hooked up, Carnivore can search through e-mail traffic in a variety of ways — by names on To and From lines, by IP address and by filtering for keywords within the header or body of an e-mail. In its description of Carnivore, the FBI insists that its software was designed to spy with "surgical" precision on specific individuals.

But Carnivore's critics are not so sure. They say that once the device is hooked up to an ISP's network, it can be used to do keyword searches — for, say, "hijack" or "Hamas" — on every e-mail that passes through. "They're sucking on the hose," says Lee Tien, senior staff attorney with the Electronic Freedom Foundation. "It's conceivable they're taking every bit and deciding whether they're entitled to it or not, but maybe they're looking at every bit."

Just what information the FBI can collect depends on what kind of court order the agency has. For phone wiretaps, the easy orders to get are "trap-and-traces," which let police record the phone numbers a suspect dials, and "pen-registers," which let them log the phone numbers of incoming calls. Those same court orders are issued for Carnivore, to get e-mail addresses. To gain access to the substance of an e-mail, the FBI needs a full-blown content wiretap, which, on the Internet as on phone lines, courts are far more wary about granting.

When Carnivore was first introduced, civil libertarians hoped to stop it. But after EarthLink lost its court case, and as there was no groundswell of popular opposition, privacy advocates increasingly redirected their efforts to halting what they see as abuses in how the FBI deploys Carnivore. "We're not trying to stop them from doing their jobs," says Ari Schwartz, a policy analyst at the Center for Democracy & Technology. "What we're talking about is oversight."

These critics would like to be sure that when Carnivore is installed on an ISP its data collection really is surgical, and that the FBI is not downloading information about nontargets it happens to intercept. They also say the FBI is misusing pen-registers and trap-and-traces. The government has argued that those limited wiretaps entitle it to e-mail headers—the headlines at the top of a message that often summarize the contents. To get access to headers, Carnivore's critics say, the FBI should have to meet the high standard for a content wiretap. They would also like to see rules that require the FBI to throw out collected evidence once an investigation is over, rather than storing it in a permanent database.

Privacy advocates say they will keep fighting these battles—before judges, in Congress and in the media. But they also realize it's suddenly a hard time to try to rein in the Carnivorous beast. "No matter how you feel about Carnivore, if the smoke is still coming off the World Trade Center, no one is going to tell the FBI they can't install it," says Dave McClure, president of the U.S. Internet Industry Association.

It's a good bet that there will be a lot more Carnivores installed in the weeks and months ahead. After Sept. 11, the FBI reportedly fanned out and installed Carnivore on ISPs around the country, without opposition.

The new national mood is also likely to give a boost to an even more sweeping eavesdropping system: Echelon, the National Security Agency's top-secret global wiretapping network. Echelon reportedly grew out of a 1945 agreement to share information obtained by bugging other countries, particularly the Soviet Union. It was developed, and is now operated, as a joint effort of the NSA and the intelligence operations of England, Canada and New Zealand. Echelon has been shrouded in mystery, so much so that its very existence was long doubted. But a report by the European Parliament in July confirmed that it is real, and that it is capable of intercepting virtually any telephone conversation, e-mail, Internet connection or fax worldwide. Echelon is believed to work like a global police scanner, and it is reportedly able to search out specific keywords like "hijack" or "bomb." Its biggest stumbling block is said to be just how much data it collects—as many as 3 million messages a minute, the European Parliament report estimated—that must then be sorted through. Clearly, if Echelon was working before Sept. 11, it didn't help.

The ACLU and other privacy advocates have long fought Echelon. Among their concerns is that because Internet traffic takes such roundabout paths, Echelon will be used to spy on Americans, even though they are outside the NSA's jurisdiction. But the NSA, which has reportedly had to lobby Congress hard for Echelon funding, will now have a far more receptive audience. Included in the items likely to be high on the NSA's wish list: funding to hire large numbers of staff, especially more Arabic speakers, to sift through data.

The terrorist attacks will also probably increase the use of "computer forensics," detective work that turns criminals' own computers against them. One of the hottest tools in the field right now is keystroke logging—law enforcement's surreptitious installation of software, or even a rigged keyboard, to log every keystroke a suspect types into his computer. Computer forensic techniques are usually kept under wraps, but keystroke logging has become public in the trial of Nicodemo S. Scarfo, an accused New Jersey bookmaker. The FBI used keystroke logging to learn the password to an encryption program Scarfo allegedly used to relay gambling and loan-sharking data. Keystroke logging is hard for law enforcement to employ because it's usually a "black-bag job"—an agent actually has to show up and install it. But it may prove to be a critical way of learning what terrorist networks are plotting before an attack actually occurs.

At the same time, some of the privacy alarms that went off after the World Trade Center attack now appear to have been false. In the hours after the attack, there were scattered reports that several anonymous proxies—services that allow users to surf the Internet or send e-mail without revealing their identity—voluntarily shut down or cut back on services. Privacy advocates were concerned that the government might start to force anonymous proxies to stop operating, in the name of national security.

But so far, no evidence has emerged that the terrorists used anonymizers. In fact, they may have intentionally avoided them. "If you're a terrorist, your main goal is not to be noticed at all," says Lance Cottrell, president of Anonymizer.com. "Using an anonymizer gets you noticed." Investigators now believe some of the hijackers accessed the Internet through computers in public libraries in Florida and Virginia. Those PCs offered them anonymity because they do not require logons or passwords, sign-in sheets are thrown out at the end of the day, and at least some of the computers had "shields" that prevented other patrons from reading what was on the screen.

Immediately after the Sept. 11 attacks, when rumors were rampant that the terrorists had encrypted their e-mail messages, it appeared that there would be a crackdown on encryption programs. Senator Judd Gregg (R., N.H.) began drawing up legislation that would require encryption programs to contain a "backdoor" that would be accessible to U.S. law enforcement. But the anti-encryption campaign gained little momentum.

In part, it was because law enforcement began to doubt that the terrorists had bothered to use encryption. But just as important, the last attempt to crack down on encryption, during the Clinton Administration, was abandoned when even its supporters began to doubt it would help. One key flaw: there's no way for the U.S. to ensure that every encryption program sold in the world has a backdoor accessible to American law enforcement. "Why would terrorists use encryption with a backdoor we had access to?" asks Dorothy Denning, a Georgetown University computer-science professor who has abandoned her past support for rules requiring backdoors. "There are a lot of good encryption companies outside the U.S. they could go to."

Besides, there's little evidence that terrorists even use encryption. Brian Gladman, who once headed up electronic security for Britain's Ministry of Defense and NATO, argues that the Sept. 11 attackers probably did not, because encrypted messages would have stood out and been more likely to have been picked up by the NSA. In fact, investigators are beginning to suspect that bin Laden's network may have moved beyond encryption to the more potent steganography, a technique that allows a message to be hidden in a music file or on a pornographic picture on a website. Steganographic messages do not need to be encrypted—they are hidden in plain sight in the vastness of cyberspace.

In the wake of the attacks, the Internet community braced for a truly draconian privacy crackdown. Cottrell heard talk of requiring Internet users to have an Internet ID card, with a smart-card reader or bio-optic identification, to go online, or imposing an affirmative duty on ISPs to track their users. Richard Smith, chief technology officer of the Brookline, Mass.-based Privacy Foundation, talked of his fears that the government would require websites to log and save visitor IP addresses, and ISPs to save e-mail, for a period of years.

There will almost certainly be some changes on the margins in privacy on the Internet. There will likely be more e-mail and Internet monitoring of specific suspects, pursuant to court orders. Echelon is likely to spy more than ever on overseas communications. And ISPs and other

Internet players will approach requests from law enforcement with a different attitude. "In the old days it was easy to take a stand and say anything goes on our ISP," says McClure. "Now they're going to be quicker to say, 'unless there's a reason to think you're breaking the law.'" Still, even most privacy advocates agree the changes won't be overwhelming. "There seem to be a lot of voices out there saying, 'Wait a minute, take this a little slower,'" says Cottrell. "We don't want to trample our civil liberties, particularly if there's no gain."

Civil libertarians argue, in fact, that as the war on terrorism continues, there could even be a renewed appreciation for privacy. After all, secrecy can also help the good guys. Anonymizer.com is making its service available for free to investigators. That will allow law enforcement at all levels to look at terrorist websites without tipping off the groups that they're being watched.

And there's another group that has traditionally relied on privacy: informants. Anonymizer.com has created a special gateway to the FBI website where anonymous tips can be left about bin Laden and his terror network. It's something legislators may want to keep in mind when they reconsider the laws of cyberspace in the days ahead. Private e-mail, anonymized Web surfing and encrypted messages can hide not only terrorists but the wavering member of their network summoning up the courage to turn them in.

B *The Right to Due Process and Military Tribunals*

·················

Peter J. Wallison

In Favor of Military Tribunals

The protests over the president's decision to authorize military tribunals to try terrorists call to mind Barry Goldwater's remark that "extremism in defense of liberty is no vice."

Peter J. Wallison is a resident fellow at the American Enterprise Institute. He was counsel to the president in the Reagan administration.

Stripping away the name-calling about kangaroo courts and star chambers, most of the arguments seem to be that there is only one way to conduct a trial, no matter what the offense and despite the fact that the Supreme Court in the past has not found these special tribunals to be inconsistent with the Constitution.

This inflexible approach is, in a way, as extreme as the views that condone terrorism itself, and the consequences of adopting it would ultimately help terrorism achieve its purposes. A little thought will reveal the problem the president confronts. Bringing Osama bin Laden and his henchmen to justice in a US court could require the government to reveal sensitive intelligence information, which could make it difficult to stop other terrorists. Yet without the information gained through intelligence sources, it could be impossible to convince a jury that these criminals and terrorists are guilty beyond a reasonable doubt.

Even in revealing secret intelligence, it may not be possible to meet the standards of a US criminal court for convicting Mr. bin Laden or his co-conspirators. When the criminal justice system deals with organized crime, it is frequently unable to gain convictions without the testimony of someone who has direct knowledge of the culpability of the Mafia boss.

That's why the traditional method of reaching the top of a crime organization is to convict those lower down and work up the chain with testimony of those already convicted or in jeopardy of conviction. These witnesses can provide evidence that a person ordered a crime, even though he did not actually perform the criminal act. This doesn't always work; witnesses may not be willing to talk or there may be none. Al Capone was famously convicted only of tax evasion, when he probably ordered many murders.

The inability to convict a criminal does not mean he is innocent. We have set the standards for conviction very high, because, in balancing society's risks against the risk of punishing an innocent person, we would rather let the guilty go free than convict the innocent. That is a policy with which few in a civilized society will quarrel, but we should recognize it as striking a balance between two competing objectives.

Should the same balance apply to trying terrorists? To answer this, it's necessary to distinguish between criminal and terrorist acts. Although there are exceptions, almost all criminal acts injure or kill relatively few people; they are carried out for reasons that we can connect to human impulses, such as greed or anger. We have a sense, then, that such acts are relatively rare, that we can take practical steps to reduce the chances that we will be victimized, and that society's risks are to some degree limited.

Acts of terrorism, however, are more than criminal acts; they are intended to kill or injure many people, more or less at random, simply to induce fear. Under these circumstances, when confronted by terrorism we must ask whether it is still good policy to let the guilty go free for fear of punishing the innocent.

Here, it seems sensible instead to strike a different balance—one that puts greater weight on protection of society than on protection of an alleged criminal's rights. If we have evidence that a person may be responsible for ordering an act that killed thousands, it makes no sense to let him go free—so he can do it again—because we don't have sufficient evidence to convict him beyond a reasonable doubt.

Thus, the issue is stark. Inflexible advocates of using the criminal courts must be willing to see some terrorists go free if there is insufficient evidence to convict. That's how our criminal justice system is intended to work, and that's the result it will inevitably produce. Those who advocate this should have the burden of demonstrating why society should be interested in striking this balance. To date, they have failed to recognize that there is a balance; they appear to believe that only the American civil jury can produce justice.

But this is surely wrong. We don't know how the terrorist trials will be conducted; trials that do not meet the standards of criminal trials are not for that reason kangaroo courts. American military officers sworn to do justice are not likely to be less fair than civil juries. It is not even clear that the trials will be wholly secret, only that the portions presenting evidence based on intelligence sources will be closed.

It has been said that the Constitution is not a suicide pact. The president's proposal shows us that, within constitutional constraints, we have the flexibility and capacity to do justice to terrorists and to ourselves.

George P. Fletcher

War and the Constitution

The media are awash in disinformation about military tribunals. Since November 13, when President George W. Bush issued his controversial executive order mandating the use of military commissions to prosecute suspected terrorists, one far-fetched claim of law has followed another. The president's lawyers have every right to put the best possible light on their plans for sidestepping the criminal courts. My problem is with the academic lawyers whose offhand opinions fill the op-ed pages and the ears of Congress. Their din reached its climax when two important legal scholars—Laurence Tribe of Harvard and Cass Sunstein of the University of Chicago—testified as "liberals" before the Senate Judiciary Committee that Bush's tribunals would be compatible with the Constitution. Of course, everybody these days is responding under pressure, but the law professors have been giving "shooting from the hip" a bad name.

Any serious examination of the sources—statutes and Supreme Court cases—should lead a fair-minded scholar to the opposite conclusion: There is no law available to support the proposed Bush tribunals. Leave aside whether the tribunals would be good or bad, kangaroo courts or simply streamlined procedure; the president has no authority to create them.

Tribe argued recently in *The New Republic* that "in wartime, 'due process of law,' both linguistically and historically, permits trying unlawful combatants for violation of the laws of war, without a jury." This single sentence captures many of the mistakes that run, like viruses, through the debate in the press. But let us begin with the fundamental question of whether the Constitution, as Tribe suggests, is different in wartime versus peacetime. In the words of the Supreme Court's 1866 ruling *Ex parte Milligan*, the leading precedent on this issue: "[T]he Constitution was intended for a state of war, as well as a state of peace, and is equally binding upon rulers and people at all times and under all circumstances." When the Sixth Amendment mandates that in "all criminal prosecutions" certain rights should apply, including the right to a jury trial, the framers mean what they say. And the Supreme Court has understood the injunction. It is undisputed law that if the civilian courts are open and functioning, the armed forces cannot convene a military commission or tribunal to try offenses that fall within the civilian courts' jurisdiction.

True, Chief Justice William H. Rehnquist wrote in his 1998 book *All the Laws but One* that in the time of a declared war the government has greater authority to infringe civil liberties. For example, the government can deport enemy aliens. But these infringements on the status of enemy aliens do not affect their right to be tried in civilian court for committing a crime in the United States. The fact of "wartime" does not change the meaning or scope of due process—either linguistically or historically.

The second basic point that we should clarify in order to think straight about criminal justice à la Bush and Attorney General John

Ashcroft concerns "unlawful combatants"—the term that Tribe uses to explain the category of people that can be tried by simplified procedures for "violation of the laws of war." This phrase, "unlawful combatant," appears all over the place as though it could be the talisman that saves Bush's tribunals.

The Supreme Court first used the term in 1942 in *Ex parte Quirin* to solve a particular problem that arose when eight German spies landed in civilian clothes on the beaches of Long Island. The FBI arrested them before they executed any of their planned acts of sabotage. President Franklin D. Roosevelt was resolved to prosecute them for something, and it turned out that there was a suitable law on the books—a provision of the U.S. Code prohibiting spying in wartime near or around American military installations. That statute required trial by either court-martial or military tribunal and imposed an automatic penalty of death. Roosevelt quickly established the military tribunal that the statute authorized, but the constitutional dilemma remained. To see it, we have to concentrate on one horn at a time.

The first problem was that these spies were members of the German army. We were at war with Germany and therefore the eight captives were arguably just like soldiers who might have crossed the Canadian border in tanks. And if they were combatants, then by the rules of international law we were not entitled to try them for acts committed in the pursuit of legitimate aims of war. As Chief Justice Harlan Fiske Stone wrote for the Supreme Court in *Quirin*: "Lawful combatants are subject [only] to capture and detention as prisoners of war by opposing military forces." The reason for this rule lies in the general understanding that a soldier is simply a servant of the state. He does not do anything in his own name. He cannot be held personally liable for the ravages of war.

Now, admittedly, there are various ways around the rule. One is to deny that the military engagement is a war and call it instead some kind of police action. But the danger of trying too hard to deny the combatant status of those engaged in military battle is that we then encounter the second horn of the dilemma: If these are merely criminals who have committed crimes against the United States, they must be tried in a federal district court. That is the holding in the 1866 decision *Milligan*. In fact, it seems to be the tack taken by Harvard University law professor Anne-Marie Slaughter, who argued against Bush's tribunals in *The New York Times*, saying that al-Qaeda members fighting in Afghanistan are really just "common criminals" and shouldn't be dignified with the status of combatants.

Here, then, was the quandary faced by the Supreme Court in 1942: Either the eight German spies were combatants or they had to be tried in federal district court—with full procedural protections—for their apparent conspiracy to commit sabotage. To find a way out of this predicament, the Court invented the category of "unlawful combatant." Eureka! The spies fell conveniently between the stools of international law (no trial for combatants) and the rule in *Milligan* (an obligatory trial in available civilian courts); thus, they could be tried in Roosevelt's tribunal. The soldiers were "unlawful" because they wore civilian clothes when they slipped behind enemy lines to spy. They did not deserve to be treated as combatants exempt from prosecution because by virtue of their deception they had not run the risk that all combatants run, namely of being shot when they cross into enemy territory.

But if there is one idea that those now commenting on Bush's proposed tribunals systematically distort, this is it. They use the word "unlawful" as if it were the equivalent of "violating the laws of war." Recall Tribe's line: "In wartime, 'due process of law' . . . permits trying unlawful combatants for violation of the laws of war." His logic seems to be that any soldier who commits a war crime would be an unlawful combatant and subject to trial by military tribunal.

Alberto Gonzales, the chief White House counsel, betrayed the same root mistake when he addressed the American Bar Association in late November. He tried to demonstrate the limited scope of the tribunals by saying that the administration was only after "enemy soldiers." Then someone reminded him that enemy soldiers are protected by the Geneva Conventions and cannot be prosecuted at all. He corrected himself by saying that tribunals were after "unlawful combatants." He, too, seems to believe that the category of "unlawful combatant" is so broad that it includes anyone the administration might want to prosecute in a special tribunal—anyone who has done something unlawful and is a combatant. But that is not the meaning of the *Quirin* precedent.

Much of the confusion arises from the failure to recognize that there are two bodies of law—both called "the law of war." To understand the difference between them, we have to think ourselves back into the period before the Nuremberg trials, before the Japanese war-crime trials, when the law of war was not primarily about crimes; it was about how you conducted yourself as someone embedded in a chain of command and therefore qualified for the immunity from prosecution promised to combatants. It meant, among other things, that you had to wear a uniform, fight with your company, and cease fighting when the army surrendered.

During World War II, the "law of war" came to refer primarily to war crimes that violated basic principles of morality and decency. But when the *Quirin* case was decided, that transformation had not yet become apparent. There was nothing immoral—by contemporary standards—about the Germans spying in the United States. The Americans would surely have done the same thing in enemy territory (and probably did if they were smart). Perhaps there was something duplicitous about crossing enemy lines in civilian clothes, but one could hardly imagine bringing a case to The Hague on those grounds. *Quirin* did not incorporate the universal standards of morality that we now associate with the principles of the Geneva Conventions and the Rome Statute of July 1998 proposing an International Criminal Court.

The key case in the transition to the modern law of war was the 1946 appeal to the U.S. Supreme Court by the Japanese General Tomoyuki Yamashita. A military tribunal in the Philippines, established by the postwar commander of the islands, Lieutenant General Wilhelm Styer, had charged Yamashita for allowing his troops to go on a rampage and commit atrocities against local civilians. The military tribunal had invented a new war crime that amounted, in effect, to a commander's negligent supervision of his troops, and the Supreme Court affirmed that it could do so. Thus was born the idea of a war crime under the law of war.

If President Bush had a precedent on his side of the argument, it would be *Yamashita v. Styer*. According to this case, he surely has the power to use tribunals to prosecute war crimes (in the modern sense) that—like the atrocities in the Philippines—occur entirely outside the jurisdiction of the United States courts. Anyone who looks into the *Yamashita* case, however, will find that it stands together with *Korematsu v. United States*, the 1944 decision upholding the military internment of American Japanese, as one of the disgraceful episodes of World War II jurisprudence. Among other things, the *Yamashita* decision violated the Geneva Convention of 1929, which provides that prisoners of war may be convicted and sentenced "only by the same courts and according to the same procedure as in the case of persons belonging to the armed forces of the detaining Power."

In other words, General Yamashita and every foreigner suspected of a war crime should have received the same procedural protection as was available in an American court-martial. (Thus, under the Geneva Conventions, Bush's executive order mandating military tribunals is unacceptable because it permits, among other things, a death sentence based on a two-thirds vote, while an American court-martial requires a unanimous vote.) The weakness of the Supreme Court's reasoning in *Yamashita* is exposed in stinging dissents by Justices Frank Murphy and Wiley Rutledge.

It is not surprising, then, that in the current discussion no one invokes the precedent of *Yamashita*. But even if those who argue for the president's tribunals wanted to invoke the case, they would have to contend with the fact that General Yamashita was not subject to prosecution in the federal courts for acts committed in the Philippines against the local population. The implication of the *Yamashita* case is that Taliban and al-Qaeda fighters who are taken prisoner could be prosecuted by military tribunals (or more properly by American courts-martial) but only for war crimes committed in Afghanistan. As for suspects who allegedly participated in a conspiracy to commit the crimes of September 11, they are liable for a crime on American soil and are therefore subject to prosecution in the federal courts. In the end, *Yamashita*—whether it is still good law or not—does not help the president's case, for the precedent is limited to cases beyond the competence of the American civilian courts.

To return, however, to the two different meanings of the law of war, what we've seen since World War II is a remarkable shift in emphasis from the law of war as a set of rules about fair fighting to the law of war *crimes* as a set of norms about decent behavior toward civilians and prisoners of war. And those who argue in favor of the president's tribunals typically confound the two. Because military tribunals do have jurisdiction over unlawful combatants, as the *Quirin* decision established, proponents claim that military tribunals can prosecute war crimes, or violations of the law of war in the modern sense. For example, in his testimony to the Senate Judiciary Committee, Cass Sunstein cited *Quirin* as though it were sufficient in itself to establish the constitutionality of Bush's tribunals.

Here is how Ruth Wedgwood, a Yale University law professor, defended the president's order in *The Wall Street Journal*: "Military courts are the traditional venue for enforcing violations of the law of war." The statement is true if she is talking about *Quirin*-type violations of the law but grossly misleading if the focus is on war crimes in the modern sense. There is no tradition or constitutional authority legitimating trial by a military tribunal when the crime is subject to prosecution under American law and the appropriate American courts are open and functioning. And ever since the postwar period, anyone suspected of a grave breach of the Geneva Conventions against American nationals is, by law, subject to prosecution in a federal district court.

One of the more disconcerting aspects of Tribe's testimony to the Senate Judiciary Committee is that he preached congressional approval as a way of remedying the defects in the Bush executive order. It never occurred to him, apparently, that Congress has no clear constitutional basis for adding to the very limited categories of crimes committed under American law that can be prosecuted in military tribunals.

In fact, the Bill of Rights guarantees a civilian court trial to anyone accused of crimes in violation of federal statutes, with only two historically entrenched exceptions. One is court-martial jurisdiction over the U.S. armed forces and the other is the limited case of spying upheld in the *Quirin* case. (*Yamashita* does not count here because it attaches to crimes committed outside the jurisdiction of American courts.) The narrow exception for court-martial jurisdiction is made explicit in the Fifth Amendment ("except in cases arising in the land or naval forces"), and the Supreme Court justified the narrow exception for the spying statute on the ground that military tribunals for spying functioned before the nation's founding and therefore were "grandfathered" into the Constitution.

Contrary to Sunstein's testimony, there is no general exception recognized in American law for war crimes committed against civilians. In fact, since World War II, all war crimes committed by U.S. troops or against American nationals have been federal offenses subject to the jurisdiction of the federal courts. Nor can you make the *Quirin* argument that jurisdiction over these crimes antedates the Constitution, for there were no war crimes (in the post-Nuremberg sense) at the time and there was certainly no war crime based on attacks against the civilian population. Also, it is worth noting that in the language of the spying statute—which provides the only congressionally authorized military tribunal to date—Congress took pains to bring the crime within the framework of court-martial jurisdiction. The offense is described in the statute as "lurking as a spy" in or around a military facility. This falls within the penumbra of court-martial jurisdiction over military bases.

The arguments concerning congressional authority do not satisfy. And if there is a good argument for the president's having inherent authority to establish the tribunals, I have yet to hear it. Ruth Wedgwood made a stunningly inaccurate claim in *The Wall Street Journal* that the president has implied power as commander in chief to set up military tribunals. She said this principle is "acknowledged by Chief Justice Stone in a 1942 opinion." The opinion she was referring to is—once again—the *Quirin* case, and here is what the chief justice actually wrote: "It is unnecessary for present purposes to determine to what extent the President as Commander in Chief has constitutional power to create military commissions without the support of Congressional legislation." Who knows what she could have been thinking.

Wedgwood also claimed that Congress has already "agreed" to the president's power to invoke military tribunals. This, too, is false. The most Congress has ever done is recognize the possible existence of military tribunals. For instance, a provision of the 1950 Universal Code of Military Justice recognizes the authority of the executive branch to prescribe rules of evidence for military courts, including existing and authorized military tribunals. But that law does not grant the president authority to convene tribunals, and it specifies no criteria as to when a tribunal should hear a case that would otherwise go to the regular civilian courts.

The fact is that the president has no apparent authority to convene military tribunals for the crimes of September 11. Of course, we do not know the circumstances in which the Defense Department will try to invoke this power to sentence supposed international terrorists to death. When it does, though, we can be sure that there will be litigation; and if the Supreme Court reads its own cases faithfully, it will uphold the rule in *Ex parte Milligan* and strike down the conviction of anyone who should have been tried in federal court.

In the meantime, the very existence of the executive order of November 13 is creating an international scandal. European countries refuse to extradite suspects to us on the ground that they can be sentenced to death in summary proceedings. And an argument is in the offing that the very threat of capital punishment against "enemy soldiers," the phrase that Alberto Gonzales let slip, can constitute a war crime by the United States. According to the Rome Statute, it is a crime for one army to declare that "no quarter will be given" to the other side. Enemy soldiers, in other words, have the right to surrender without being harmed. Yet if we threaten them with the death penalty by summary proceedings, we are in effect depriving them of their right to a safe surrender and thus declaring that "no quarter will be given."

The irony is that the administration has ably pursued its war aims. In this area of demonstrating respect for the Constitution and international law, however, it has failed miserably. Perhaps that is because the Bush team has been uncertain whether they are fighting a war or trying to arrest those who financed and organized the attacks of September 11. They cannot quite decide whether this was a collective crime of al-Qaeda and the Taliban, in which case war is the proper response, or the individual crime of Osama bin Laden and other as yet unidentified individuals, in which case a criminal prosecution is the correct action. The military tribunals offer a halfway-house approach that they may see as prosecuting the war while also bringing the bad guys to justice.

Sooner or later, however, despite the failure of our "liberal" law professors, the truth will win out: The prosecution of suspects for crimes committed on American soil must—if the charges were not prosecuted in tribunals at the time of the Constitution—come before the federal courts. Neither the president nor Congress has the authority to suspend that constitutional guarantee.

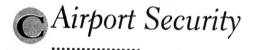 *Airport Security*

Richard W. Rahn

The Case Against Federalizing Airport Security

Would you feel safer if the security personnel at Disney World were federal government employees? Probably not, because the private companies that service Disney World and most other attractions have been doing a fine job. The amount of crime at such places is minimal, and most people correctly perceive their person and property as being perfectly safe.

The Senate has just passed a bill that would require all airport security personnel to be federal employees. Does this make any sense? If the security personnel at Boston, Newark and Dulles airports had been federal employees, would the terrorists acts of September 11 been averted? The answer is almost certainly no, because up to that date it was not illegal to carry a box cutter on an airplane.

Those who advocate federalizing the airport security personnel claim that we will be safer if the workers are paid more and are better trained. Let's assume this assertion is true. But now ask, is it necessary that they be federal employees?

Richard W. Rahn is an adjunct scholar of the Cato Institute.

Consider what would likely happen if the feds took over the airport security function. With civil service protections, it would be very difficult to fire any of them. Hence, the incentive to do a consistently outstanding job and always be courteous to harried passengers would be lacking. (Federal employees who are in more creative jobs often do very good work, but examining airline passengers' personal belongings all day is not likely to fit the category of an interesting job.) The fact is their work will be easier when fewer people fly, hence they would have an incentive to discourage people from flying rather than making it a pleasant experience.

If the federal government took over this airport security function, it would have a monopoly on the activity. We all know that monopolies are bad, because they resist innovation, result in higher costs and poorer service, and tend to engage in cover-ups for their own mistakes and deficiencies. We only need to look at the many recent failures of the F.B.I., the most elite federal police force, to have doubts about a less elite operation. The airport security service is more likely to resemble the I.N.S., which has a long record of incompetence, including the failure (along with the F.B.I.) to remove the terrorists who were here illegally.

On Oct. 15, I had an appointment with several colleagues from other think tanks to give a presentation in the U.S. Capitol building. The Capitol, understandably so, is under very tight security, and has an elite police force. When we arrived, we were put through the normal electronic security checks, and upon stating the purpose of our visit and room we were supposed to go to, we were waved through. Several minutes later we were stopped for not wearing nametags, which we had neither been issued nor asked to wear, nor had any objection to wearing. We were then escorted like miscreants back to the door where we entered. What ensued was a spectacle of several Capitol police in an extended argument with each other, in front of us, over who should wear nametags and who should not for what rooms. Ultimately, it was decided we should not wear nametags, much to the displeasure of the nametag advocate.

Shortly thereafter, one of our other colleagues joined us, and mentioned that they would not let him in the first entrance he went to, so he merely went to another entrance and freely walked in. The point here is not to beat up on the Capitol police who were all trying to do their job as they understood it under difficult circumstances, but to illustrate that a federal operating and managed police force is unlikely to be a panacea. If the elite Capitol police cannot get their act together in more than a month after the terrorist attack for one of the most important buildings in the country, why should one assume that newly hired federal security personnel in all of the nation's airports would be any more competent?

Clearly a more effective solution for the airport security problem would be for the federal government to set standards for airport security and monitor the airports to make sure the standards are being met. For instance, standards for private security personnel might include criminal background checks, a requirement that they must all be US citizens, have completed specified security training, plus a course on how to be pleasant and helpful to the passengers. Security operations at some airports have been lax and the employees rude because the contracting authorities have either not set or not enforced more rigorous standards. Sixteen European countries are reported to have replaced government security personnel with private security firms at airports with very good results, because the governments require high standards of performance.

In organized sports, we separate the rule making and refereeing functions from the playing function, for good reasons. We know in football if we allowed the referees to be part of the home team organization, that many of the mistakes of the home team might be overlooked. The principle is universal; we are likely to get much better airport security if the government sets the rules and enforces the standards on independent operators rather than undertakes the task itself. If the private security company knows that it will lose its contract and if its employees know that they will lose their jobs if they fail to meet the specified standards, there is a strong incentive for good performance that would be lacking if the government were the direct employer.

Socialism has an almost 100 percent record of failure, so why would we want to socialize an activity that clearly could be more competently managed privately?

P. W. Singer

Arguments Against Federalization Flimsy

There may be no greater sign that a return to normalcy is at hand than the good old-fashioned partisanship we saw as the House and Senate sparred over their competing bills on airport security.

Of all the areas to spark a political battle, however, this one makes the least sense. The House's reasons for not wanting a federal security force sound reasonable in theory, but they fall on their face when considering the crisis at hand.

Many opponents of federalizing security believe that if a job can be done by private business, then it should be. On Sept. 11, however, we saw the dangers of a different sort of private efficiency.

The Argenbright company (owned by a European conglomerate) provides security at 17 of the nation's 20 largest airports, including Boston's Logan, Washington's Dulles and Newark. The firm pleaded guilty last year to conspiracy and fraud charges related to its inadequate training and background checks for thousands of employees. Recent inspections at Dulles found it still has systematic problems; seven out of 20 of its screeners tested did not have the skills needed to do their jobs.

Market efficiency comes at the risk of market failures. Turning to the market induces some companies to offer leaner and more effective solutions. But it can also lead other companies to cut corners in order to earn profits, including paying their employees pitiful salaries or saving money through shoddy employment and training practices.

Given the breakdown by private security on Sept. 11 and the continuing dangers that their poor standards of performance present, it makes sense to turn this business back over to public servants, whose primary concern is the community's safety, not the bottom line.

Others in the House oppose the federalization of airport security because they fear it will expand the size of government. While rooted in common sense, this also is a red herring. Regardless of the outcome on airport security, winning the fight against terrorism will require more soldiers, more border guard inspectors and more biological warfare experts. All will be part of the government.

More importantly, there is nothing wrong with that. A strong government is not inherently bad. Rather, the danger is if it interferes in the wrong areas, such as religion or the arts. If our safety isn't the role for the government, what is?

Some politicians apparently also oppose the federalization of airport security because it might lead to more federal workers, who will be members of unions. They argue that union workers tend to perform worse and are harder to replace if they do a poor job. While we all know the stereotype of the lazy federal employee, this is no time for stereotypes.

Most of the brave police, fire and rescue personnel who died in New York were members of government employee unions.

Did this make them somehow less worthy of our respect and support? Did they do a worse job because of the professional organizations they were part of? The fact is that nonunion workers are the ones now who are not performing to the required standards.

Moreover, the problem with airport security is not a matter of getting rid of poor employees. Instead, it is the exact opposite—the incredibly high turnover within the current work force. Paid at cut-rate wages, airport security employees don't last longer than six months and thus don't build up the expertise to do their job.

At the base of these politician's fears, however, is something more pernicious. Many believe that a broadened federal union work force would be more likely to vote for one party and thus should be prevented. This idea deserves not only our scorn but censure.

Leaving aside that the small number of new employees (about 20,000) would be unlikely to swing any election, unless they were all based in Florida, the assumption that public safety should rank behind potential voting patterns is disturbing. The key is who can do a better job, not whether they tend to vote Republican or Democrat.

In the end, the choice is clear, and it is one that an overwhelming majority of the American public supports. Our airports deserve the same level of protection that the members of the House now enjoy for themselves but chose to vote against—that provided by government employees.

Let's hope bipartisan compromise will return and bring us back to reason.

Homeland Defense in a Federal System

....

Sydney J. Freedberg Jr. and Marilyn Werber Serafini

Health and Welfare: Contagious Confusion

In a way that the far bloodier September 11 attacks did not, the anthrax assault has required unprecedented collaboration: among law enforcement, emergency management, and public health officials; among federal, state, and local government; and between government at all levels and the medical community. If the attacks-by-mail did America any kind of favor, it was to highlight how many weak links there are in the chains that bind these agencies to each other in a cri-sis—links that must be strengthened before a far heavier blow breaks them apart completely.

The American public health system is decentralized and uncoor-dinated, and its response to anthrax wasn't pretty. But some lessons are being learned.

Consider **Clifford Ong**, Indiana's new statewide counter-terrorism coordinator, appointed two weeks into the crisis as the Hoosier version of national Homeland Security chief **Tom Ridge**. Ong's office, intend-ed to be the state's central clearinghouse for anthrax information, first learned about Indiana's most serious anthrax scare, not through official channels, but from the media. Although about 600 miles from any con-firmed case of anthrax, Indianapolis happens to have one of the only two facilities nationwide that repair and recycle post office sorting machines—including a tainted printer from Trenton, N.J. State authorities did not even know the repair plant was there until a sub-contractor called asking for advice about how to handle machinery pos-sibly exposed to anthrax. The state then tested for anthrax at the repair plant, and the report came back negative. Ong relaxed. But he didn't know that the main contractor at the plant had asked the U.S. Postal

Service to come and do its own test. This second test, performed by an out-of-state lab, came back positive. Suddenly, there was anthrax in Indiana, and yet state authorities weren't told. Reporters in Washington were. Ong had to field the frantic calls.

"Our problem isn't locally," said Ong, who has long worked with the local U.S. district attorney and the FBI field office. "Washington seems to respond within the Beltway to national media without any concern that we have local media. . . . It puts us in somewhat of a defensive position."

This snafu—just one of many—shows how vital information can fall into the cracks between organizations, into blind spots where fear can flourish like mold inside a wall. Considering that just four people died of anthrax in one month, the average American was far more likely to be struck by lightning, which kills 80 to 100 people every year, than to contract the disease. The point is that anthrax is not contagious—but fear is. "The medical problem was actually pretty small," said **Jack Harrald**, the director of the Institute for Crisis, Disaster, and Risk Management at George Washington University in Washington. "The terror problem, in terms of managing people's fear, was pretty huge—and not very well managed."

The failure of government, medicine, and media to respond to fears and ignorance about anthrax with real understanding led to millions of dollars in losses—to businesses that had to find substitute mail carriers or evacuate their workplaces for testing, as well as to local governments that had to respond to every emergency anthrax scare. In Los Angeles, where hazardous-materials responses increased 300 percent in mid-October, "we received a call from an employee at a doughnut shop that there's a white, powdery substance on the floor," said Deputy Chief **Darrell Higuchi**, of the Los Angeles County Fire Department. The shop, of course, sold doughnuts with powdered sugar. "Yet," said Higuchi, "you feel for the callers, because they are scared."

Fear thrives on ignorance. But there is no effective, authoritative, nationwide system to communicate information about bioterror. Nor is there a single national spokesperson for the public's health. Indeed, some have criticized the Bush Administration for failing to designate someone as the voice of the anthrax crisis, even acknowledging White House reluctance to call on Surgeon General **David Satcher**, a leftover Clinton Administration appointee. Instead, information has moved through dozens of parallel and poorly coordinated channels of communication: The Centers for Disease Control and Prevention talks to state health officers, the FBI to local sheriffs, the Federal Emergency Management Agency to disaster officials, medical associations to their members. But when people in different fields, such as police and physicians, must work together, or when there simply is no state or local counterpart to a federal agency, the channels are less clear—as Ong found out in dealing with the Postal Service. The system simply isn't set up to share information.

In fact, civil liberties laws often forbid necessary communication. Said **Lawrence Gostin**, the director of the Center for Law and the Public's Health, a joint project of Georgetown University and Johns Hopkins University: "The law thwarts vital information-sharing vertically from federal to state, and horizontally between law enforcement, emergency management, and public health."

The biggest gap is between government and the medical community. A CDC alert on bioterrorism, sent to state health officials just after September 11, had still not reached many local emergency rooms a week later. And the crucial linchpins between doctors and officials—local public health offices—are notoriously overworked and short of funds. As many as one in five public health offices do not even have e-mail, said Sen. **Bill Frist**, R-Tenn., a physician. Many localities still collect epidemiological data on disease outbreaks only by asking doctors to send postcards through the mail—hardly an ideal approach in any fast-moving outbreak, let alone one that strikes at the postal system.

Anthrax has finally kick-started efforts to revive public health systems, after decades of neglect. In North Carolina, for example, the Legislature is about to allocate millions of dollars to replace reporting by postcard with high-speed, highly secure electronic links. Ultimately, the network will connect not only local officials, but also every hospital, pharmacy, and doctor's office in the state.

New funding and new networks are essential first steps. But in a country where almost all health care is provided by the private sector—indeed, where most critical terrorist targets, from Internet servers to nuclear plants to sports arenas, are privately owned—defense against terrorism probably cannot be achieved by a new agency, a new program, or a new technology. True "homeland security," most experts say, will require an overarching system that links not just every level and agency of government, but also the private sector, nonprofit groups, and the general public. Computers and the Internet will be vital in helping to set up this new national network, but it will be the intangible connections between people working together in a common cause that will really make the new system work.

The Broken Linchpin

If it sometimes seems as if the world has turned upside down since September 11, that's because it has. Terrorism has upset the traditional pyramid of who protects whom. No longer do the Pentagon's armed troops bear the brunt of foreign blows. Whether the danger comes from airliners-as-bombs or from anthrax envelopes, local firefighters, medics, and police respond long before Washington can act. But even the local emergency teams come second to the scene. In a terrorist attack, the first responder is the ordinary citizen—the airline passenger who decides to rush the hijackers, the mailroom clerk who notices a suspicious package, or anyone who wonders whether these flu-like symptoms they're feeling might be anthrax. It is their decisions, prudent or paranoid, that trigger the government response. Said **Peter Probst**, a former Pentagon and CIA official, "The first line of defense is an educated, engaged public."

That word, "educated," signals where things start breaking down. Even those officials who should be best equipped to inform have stumbled over their own statements, and each other's—and that includes Surgeon General Satcher and Health and Human Services Secretary **Tommy G. Thompson**.

"You've got Satcher saying one thing, Tommy Thompson saying another, and the CDC saying a third," fumed one local official who spoke with *National Journal*. One day the word is to put everyone on Cipro, the next day not, the third day it's another antibiotic altogether. "There isn't a consistent message."

With that confusion at the top, many officials, never mind ordinary citizens, admit turning to the news media as their first source of knowledge. But as reporters themselves grope in the dark for information, and constantly face the pressure for round-the-clock, up-to-the-minute coverage, they may magnify inconclusive clues, or even outright rumors, into major scare stories. There was so much misinformation about anthrax early on, said one congressional staffer well versed in bioterror, "the first few days, I was kicking the television a lot."

Many confused citizens dialed 911, just to be sure. Far more fell back on the second line of defense: their doctors. Physicians are still trusted more than most other professionals. And even though only a handful of American doctors have ever seen a case of inhalation anthrax (the last U.S. case was in 1978), most rushed to learn what they could. Until recently, medical education on bioweapons has been minimal. But after September 11, well before the first anthrax case in

Florida, sensitivity to terror of all kinds was so high that the major medical associations quickly rallied to upload data to their Web sites and downlink teleconferences to their members.

That information probably saved lives. Had Florida photo editor **Bob Stevens** died in August, said **Randall Larsen**, director of the Anser Institute for Homeland Security, a consulting group in Northern Virginia, "it's highly unlikely he would have been diagnosed as dying with anthrax, because they weren't looking for it." Before September 11, when authorities sent anthrax samples to four medical laboratories as a test of their bioterrorism alertness, three of the labs just threw the samples out, mistaking the anthrax bacteria for contamination on the slides. In another test, out of a roomful of doctors at Johns Hopkins medical center, just one recognized an X-ray of a strange chest inflammation as characteristic of anthrax. Even after the September 11 attacks, HHS Secretary Thompson initially suggested that Stevens's death was due to a freak natural cause. But doctors were on high enough alert by then to spot the symptoms.

Although the professional medical associations could deluge their members with basic references on anthrax, they lacked the quick communications systems to collect and broadcast up-to-date data on the ever-changing outbreak. In fact, since most associations serve only a single medical specialty—and even the mighty American Medical Association serves fewer than half of all doctors—they could not even help share information among different types of doctors in a given community.

The painstaking, county-by-county collation of data gathered from individual physicians has always fallen to local public health offices— the traditional American defensive line against disease. But emergency officials, medical associations, and independent experts alike all agree that the public health infrastructure has long been, to quote one congressional staffer, "the forgotten stepchild." These local offices are perpetually short on funds, technology, and—above all—personnel. They are burdened with laws written to guard against 19th-century scourges such as syphilis and tuberculosis, and few of these laws even require doctors to report outbreaks of likely bioweapons such as anthrax, much less the subtler indications of spreading disease.

"Suppose there's a run on anti-diarrhea medication. How would we know that? If there are a lot of absences from school or work, how would we know that?" said Georgetown University's Gostin. "We need a public health agency to be able to get information from the private sector."

New York City, considered a national model, does keep hourly tabs on such things as sales of the anti-diarrheal Kaopectate. Los Angeles hospitals are linked by computer to share diagnosis data. But most areas lack such sophisticated "disease surveillance" systems, even in states that have really tried. Virginia, for example, connects its local health offices across the state by computer, said **George Foresman**, a Virginia emergency management official, but the state's effort to bring private practices into the network stalled because "we just had not been able to secure the funding."

The problems are not only fiscal. Even with a $1.4 million federal grant, Michigan found the private sector deeply reluctant to share information. "We've asked pharmacies if we could monitor what antibiotics are going out," said Dr. **Sandro Cinti**, of the University of Michigan medical center, "but they didn't want to give away that information."

In the absence of even such imperfect electronic systems, most public health officials collect data the old-fashioned way: slowly. In some places, doctors' offices fill out and mail in forms to health agencies; in other places, they call in, and local officials must laboriously enter the information by hand, and then in turn mail another piece of paper to the state health office. Conversely, when Illinois authorities, who have invested heavily in linking public health offices to local hospitals, wanted to send every physician in the state advice on anthrax, they had to take the licensing board's master list of addresses and mail every one of them a letter. There was no comprehensive e-mail or electronic system.

"The information-gathering and decision-making loop isn't fast enough," said **Clark Staten**, the executive director of the Emergency Response & Research Institute in Chicago. "The bad guys can move faster than the good guys—at the present time." And during that lag, fear can spread, and people can die.

More Than Medical

Even in a better-than-average flu season, doctors may run out of vaccine and hospitals out of beds. In some cities last year, said Sen. Edward Kennedy, D-Mass., "they had sick patients that couldn't even be treated in the emergency rooms—they were out in cars."

Any major natural disease outbreak overtaxes American medicine. But biological terrorism takes the complexity an octave higher. Each scattering of spores is obviously a public health problem. But it is also evidence of a crime—and of a hazardous material in the environment. Anthrax not only requires close "vertical" cooperation among federal, state, local, and private medical organizations, it also cuts horizontally across functional lines. Ordinary disease can be dropped neatly into an organizational box marked "medical." Bioterrorism requires out-of-the-box cooperation among public health professionals, private doctors, law enforcement agencies, firefighters, emergency management systems, and even foreign intelligence agencies.

This kind of jurisdiction-crossing is so alien to American government that it is often outright illegal. If the Central Intelligence Agency had somehow found out beforehand about the anthrax-laced letter addressed to Senate Majority Leader Thomas A. Daschle, for example, it may not have been allowed to warn health officials until after it was sent, according to **James Hodge**, the project director of the Center for Law and Public's Health. To protect civil liberties, said Hodge, "there's a firewall between intelligence agencies and public health."

Even when there's no legal obstacle to collaboration, many of the various agencies lack the experience, the contacts, or the procedures to work together. Both the U.S. Postal Inspection Service and the Centers for Disease Control are trying to track the anthrax letters to their source. The two agencies share information, but they don't share people: Instead of combining forces, detectives and doctors are on two separate teams following different methods to reach the same goal.

Sometimes, the lack of coordination could have even worse consequences. "When I was the health commissioner of New York, I had no clue who was the head of the FBI office, and he had no clue who I was," said **Margaret Hamburg**, who went on to become HHS's top bioterror official under **President Clinton**. "The last thing they want to be doing is exchanging business cards in the middle of a crisis." Yet, that is just what often happened with the anthrax scare.

In the District of Columbia, for instance, where traditional federal-local complications compounded all the other problems, the initial confusion and inconsistencies in testing and treatment for Capitol Hill staff versus postal workers boiled over into racially tinged fury. One community forum turned, unfairly, into a pillorying of D.C. public health chief **Ivan Walks**. Soon Dr. Walks and Mayor **Anthony Williams** were holding joint press conferences with Postal Service officials and the CDC. But those relationships had to be set up on the spot—and the public health office still does not have a full-time representative in the District's interagency Emergency Operations Center.

D.C.'s problem is not uncommon. "We somehow managed to leave the public health system... outside the emergency system," said

Harrald, at D.C.'s George Washington University. Emergency managers, firefighters, and police have largely overcome past problems of coordination by planning and training together before disasters, and by jointly staffing command posts during times of crisis. Such a combined system cranked into action in New York City on September 11. "The federal government had thousands of people moving in the right direction 20 minutes after the second tower was hit," Harrald said. "We know how to do this. That's the good news."

The bad news is that, in most places, no one told public health officials the good news. In D.C., "it took a long time before the emergency room at [George Washington University] hospital and the emergency room at Children's Hospital and the attending physician of the Capitol and the CDC had the same picture of what they were dealing with," Harrald said. "I'm not throwing stones at individuals. The problem is that we didn't set the systems up before the event."

The American Answer

In the first month of anthrax attacks, the country's system of defenses against bioterror often seemed to be no system at all, only chaos. Fortunately, reality is more nuanced, and more heartening, than that. True, there is no one coherent national system. But there are systems — all partial, all imperfect, but needing mainly to be strengthened and brought into an overarching structure. Senate Health, Education, Labor, and Pensions Committee Chairman Kennedy and panel member Frist last year co-sponsored the Public Health Threats and Emergencies Act of 2000, which authorized $540 million a year to strengthen the public health infrastructure and to better recognize and respond to bioterrorism attacks. Congress has not yet funded the new law, but already the two Senators have upped their request to $1.4 billion a year.

The final sum needed for homeland security will surely be much higher. But "we're not going to create a whole new Department of Defense," with a $350 billion budget and staff of 3 million, said **David McIntyre** of the Anser Institute. "We're going to play with the chips that are on the table."

"The pieces are there," said Frist. The task is taking the pieces that exist—federal, state, local, and private—"and coordinating them in a seamless way. It can be done." In Frist's own field, transplant surgery, moving precious organs quickly across the country and then ensuring that patients' bodies do not reject the new tissue require far-flung hospitals and diverse disciplines to work closely together—and they do it, every day.

High on Capitol Hill's agenda is a massive reinvestment in the nation's long-neglected public health system. Top priority is a secure, high-speed electronic data-link for doctors and public health officials who are now scrawling disease reports on postcards. The CDC already has an electronic Epidemic Information Exchange system to share outbreak alerts among federal, state, and local public health officials, as well as the military. And long before September 11, the CDC had given all 50 states seed money to start work on a National Electronic Disease Surveillance System to link all 2,000-plus local health offices around the country. This network could automatically and swiftly share, for example, the results of a crucial diagnostic test. Ultimately, it could also tap into hospitals and even private practices. But for now, the surveillance network does not actually exist. A bare-bones "base system" is scheduled to begin in 20 states in 2002. That seemed plenty fast—before September 11. Now, lawmakers are likely to hit the gas.

But strengthening public health is only half the battle, because public health officials will still get their information from the private sector. The real challenge is to track—from every hospital, every doctor's office, and every pharmacy around the country—the telltale upticks in certain symptoms, or prescriptions, that although seemingly innocuous in isolation, could signal an impending crisis. It is a daunting task.

Yet it is also mostly done already. Insurance companies routinely require doctors to code each diagnosis and report it electronically for reimbursement, keeping electronic tabs on everything from pharmaceutical sales to major surgeries. The Health Insurance Portability and Accountability Act of 1996 (HIPAA) made such reporting systems mandatory nationwide, though a significant 43 percent of doctors are not yet hooked up. In its patient-privacy rules, the act also has a little-known exception that requires doctors to share data on threats to public health.

Medical information companies are already on the Hill touting software solutions. A properly designed system could tap into the existing streams of data, strip off names and other individual identifiers, and crunch the numbers into trends. To be sure, such an early-warning system might well find false patterns. An upsurge in sales of certain drugs might indicate an outbreak of disease, or it could simply reflect effective advertising. Conversely, the system might miss a real outbreak if doctors consistently misdiagnosed as flu the ambiguous early symptoms of, say, anthrax—the reason why D.C.'s Walks is currently working on a system that codes not just final diagnoses but actual symptoms as well.

Still, the most sophisticated computer is only a tool. The most important linkages are among people. And in small ways, that linking process has already begun, too. Tom Ridge has held teleconferences with all 50 state governors. Local officials and medical associations are reaching out to one another, often through e-mail. And a FEMA program called "Project Impact" gives local governments grants and training to bring together different agencies, businesses, and community groups for disaster planning. Mayor **Susan Savage** of tornado-prone Tulsa, Okla., says that Project Impact simply but systematically asks, "What does the private sector bring to the table that can complement public resources?" On September 11, for example, when 800 airline passengers were stranded at the Tulsa airport, the city mobilized everything from public buses for transportation to local preachers for counseling, pulling resources freely from the public, private, and nonprofit sectors.

Officials, legislators, and experts increasingly agree that such bottom-up approaches are the model for homeland security. Imposing a single national system from the top down is not only impractical, it is probably unwise. What makes more sense is a "network of networks," an overarching system that lets each local government or private group tailor its approach to its own unique needs—within the overall framework.

A prototype nationwide network of networks has actually already been built. Unfortunately, it was promptly taken apart soon after. Late in 1999, when the public and private sectors alike were fretting that their computers might crash once the year hit "oo," then-Secretary of State **Madeleine K. Albright** visited the national Y2K crisis center and exclaimed, "You could really run the world from here."

Like a terrorist, the Y2K bug threatened to strike unpredictably at any target: federal, state, local, or, in the vast majority of cases, private. Imposing a top-down structure to address the potential threat was impossible, recalled **John Koskinen**, Clinton's Y2K coordinator: "You need to build off existing structures, and not create new ones." So Koskinen pulled together existing networks—government agencies, corporations, trade associations, and industry groups—in a loose but comprehensive confederation that reached into every threatened sector, with himself as the lead spokesman.

"The year-2000 preparations were a pretty good dress rehearsal" for the kind of coordination required since September 11, said **David Vaughan**, a Texas public health official. **JoAnne Moreau**, the emergency preparedness director of Baton Rouge, La., agreed: "We developed relationships with agencies and companies and factions that we never knew would have some kind of role."

The lesson that Y2K holds for homeland defense is that the federal government cannot, need not, and probably should not, do everything. Of course, without strong guidance from Washington, the thousands of private and local-government responses could create an irrational tangle, like an ill-tended garden. The federal role is to fertilize the growth and, when necessary, prune it back. "There are 1,800 separate legal jurisdictions in the United States, and the American people and the Constitution like it that way," said **David Siegrist** of the Potomac Institute for Policy Studies think tank. "The federal government needs to offer incentives... and set standards."

In a shadow war with an amorphous foe, America can prevail only by empowering individuals and small groups to innovate—because it is they, and not any federal official, who will be on the front lines. Thirtyyears ago, noted McIntyre, if a child showed up at school beaten black and blue, teachers might think, "Tough parents," and move on. Today, they would report the possible abuse—and thereby set various responses in motion. A public similarly well-educated to watch for something genuinely wrong in their world would go a long way, not just toward calming panic, but toward stopping terrorists before they strike.

"We don't want to be people who watch each other. We want to be people who watch out for each other," said McIntyre. "It's the distinction between a controlled society and a civil society. A civil society requires citizens. And in good times, maybe we forgot that."

We have certainly been reminded now.

David Carr

The Futility of "Homeland Defense"

Get over thinking that America can be made safe. Defending a country as big and commercially robust as the United States raises profound, and probably insurmountable, issues of scale. There has been much talk of "Israelifying" the United States, but America has about forty-seven times as many people as Israel, and roughly 441 times the amount of territory to be defended. New Jersey alone is 753 square miles bigger than Israel, and home to nearly 2.5 million more people. Beyond problems of size, it's all too reasonable to assume that America won't be safe. Righting various asymmetries merely designs—as opposed to prevents—the next attack. When one target is shored up, nimble transnational cells that can turn on a dime simply find new bull's-eyes. Up against those practical realities, homeland security is the national version of the gas mask in the desk drawer—something that lets people feel safer without actually making them so.

If America is riddled with holes and targets, it's because a big society designed to be open is hard to change—impossible, probably. In 2000 more than 350 million non-U.S. citizens entered the country. In 1999 Americans made 5.2 billion phone calls to locations outside the United States. Federal Express handles nearly five million packages every business day, UPS accounts for 13.6 million, and until it became a portal for terror, the Postal Service processed 680 million pieces of mail a day. More than two billion tons of cargo ran in and out of U.S. ports in 1999, and about 7.5 million North Americans got on and off cruise ships last year.

Group targets are plentiful. There are eighty-six college and professional stadiums that seat more than 60,000 people, and ten motor speedways with capacities greater than 100,000; the Indianapolis Motor Speedway seats more than 250,000. Few other countries offer the opportunity to take aim at a quarter million people at once. Also plentiful are tall buildings—until just yesterday the dominant symbol of civic pride. Fifty of the hundred tallest buildings in the world are on U.S. soil. Minneapolis, a mid-size city that doesn't leap to mind as a target, has three of them. And one of its suburbs has the largest shopping mall in the country, the Mall of America, with at least 600,000 visitors a week.

As for trained personnel to defend our borders and targets, the Immigration and Naturalization Service, which oversees the inspection of half a billion people a year, has only 2,000 agents to investigate violations of immigration law. The Postal Service has only 1,900 inspectors to investigate the misuse of mail. According to one estimate, it would take 14,000 air marshals to cover every domestic flight—more than the total number of special agents in the FBI. The former drug czar General Barry McCaffrey has pointed out that at least four different agencies oversee 303 official points of entry into the United States. After staffing increases over the past three years there are 334 U.S. Border Patrol agents guarding the 4,000 miles of Canadian border. The nation has 95,000 miles of shoreline to protect. "No one is in charge," McCaffrey says.

In all the discussion of building a homeland-security apparatus, very little attention has been paid to the fundamental question of whether 100 percent more effort will make people even one percent safer. The current version of America can no more button up its borders than mid-empire Britain could. Not just cultural imperatives are at stake. America makes its living by exporting technology and pop culture while importing hard goods and unskilled labor. The very small percentage of unwanted people and substances that arrive with all the people and things we do want is part of the cost of being America, Inc.

This is not the first time a President has declared a war within U.S. borders. In 1969 President Richard Nixon promised a "new urgency and concerted national policy" to combat the scourge of drugs—an initiative that has lurched along for more than three decades, growing to the point where the government spent $18.8 billion in 2000 trying to solve America's drug problem.

The drug war is progressing only marginally better than the one in Vietnam did. Adolescent use of most drugs has tailed off in the past year or two, but the hard-core population of 10 to 15 million American users can always find narcotics—and at a price that continues to drop. From 1981 to 1998 the price of both cocaine and heroin dropped substantially, while the purity of both drugs rose. From 1978 to 1998 the number of people dying from overdoses doubled, according to the Office of National Drug Control Policy. The Drug Enforcement Agency estimates that 331 tons of cocaine were consumed in the United States in 2000.

Counterterrorism is the ultimate zero-tolerance affair. Yet the same federal assets deployed in the war on drugs—the Coast Guard, U.S. Customs, the INS, the Border Patrol, the CIA, the FBI, and the DEA—are the first and last lines of defense in this new war. The fight against terror involves a triad that drug warriors can recite in their sleep: global source management, border interdiction, and domestic harm reduction.

In both wars human ingenuity is a relentless foe. Create a new blockade and some opportunist will survey the landscape for an alternative path. "What the war on drugs tells us," says Eric E. Sterling, of The Criminal Justice Policy Foundation, "is that people motivated by the most elementary of capitalist motives are constantly testing and finding ways to get in. Terrorists are as motivated as the most avaricious drug importer, if not more—and they are not going to be deterred by whatever barriers are put up."

Less than ten miles southwest of where the World Trade Center towers stood, the part of the Port of New York and New Jersey that occupies sections of Newark and Elizabeth is back to work. On the day I went there in October, straddle carriers—leggy, improbable contraptions that lift and cradle containers—buzzed around in the shadow of the Monet, a large cargo ship. The Monet is a floating lesson in friction-free commerce. It is operated by CMA CGM, a French company, but owned by the U.S. subsidiary of a German firm; it is registered in Monrovia, and it sails under the Liberian flag. Like everything else in view, it's massive, capable of holding 2,480 twenty-foot-long container units—the kind familiar from flatbed trucks and freight trains. It left Pusan, Korea, on September 19, stopping in three Chinese cities before sailing across the Pacific and through the Panama Canal and coming to rest in New Jersey on October 22.

The Port of New York and New Jersey is no less international. It's the busiest port on the East Coast. In 2000 the port moved approximately 70 million tons of general and bulk cargo, the equivalent of three million containers, from hundreds of cities around the globe, and half a million freshly built cars. The large containers it processes are stuffed, sealed, and tagged in far-flung locations, and their contents move, mostly unchecked, into the hands of consumers. A conga line of trains and trucks snakes out of the port, bound for a metropolitan market of some 18 million people.

Smuggling goods in containers probably started the day after shipping goods in them did. In a sting last January, U.S. Customs and the DEA seized 126 pounds of heroin concealed in twelve bales of cotton towels on a container ship at the port. That same month two men were charged with importing 3.25 million steroid pills that were seized during a customs examination of a container shipped from Moldavia. And in May of 1999 the DEA and Customs seized 100 kilograms of cocaine hidden under 40,000 pounds of bananas in two refrigerated containers. Sometimes the cargo isn't cargo at all. In October, Italian authorities found a suspected terrorist—an Egyptian-born Canadian dressed in a business suit—ensconced in a shipping container. His travel amenities included a makeshift toilet, a bed, a laptop computer, two cell phones, a Canadian passport, security passes for airports in three countries, a certificate identifying him as an airline mechanic, and airport maps. The container was headed for Toronto from Port Said, Egypt.

Before September 11 only about two percent of all the containers that move through ports were actually inspected. At Port Newark-Elizabeth there is a single giant on-site x-ray machine to see inside the containers; since September 11 two portable machines have been brought in to supplement it. The Customs Service enforcement team has been temporarily increased by 30 percent, but even that means that a mere 100 inspectors are responsible for more than 5,000 containers every day. The service has been on Alert Level One, which theoretically means that more containers are being inspected. But not even that vigilance — let alone the overtime — can continue indefinitely.

By reputation and appearance, the port is extremely well run, and it had tightened up security even before September 11. In the mid-1990s port officials began requiring every incoming truck driver to obtain an ID badge. One fall morning a man who appeared to be a Sikh, in a brilliant-orange turban and a lengthy beard, drew double takes from the other truckers — as he would anyplace else — when he stopped by the administration building to get his credential. When I was there, foreign crews were restricted from leaving their ships. The Coast Guard required ninety-six hours' notice before a ship arrived, and boarded every vessel before it was allowed into port. Two tugs accompanied each ship on its way in; if the ship were to head toward, say, a bridge support or some other target, the tugs would muscle the ship away.

But commerce, by definition, requires access. The port offers obvious targets because it is a place of business, not a fortified military installation. Tanks of edible oils sit behind a single cyclone fence; tankers of orange-juice concentrate from Brazil stand unguarded in parking lots. Two squad cars, one belonging to the port and the other on loan from the Department of Corrections, were parked at one of the port's major intersections, but anyone can drive around much of the facility without having to pass a single checkpoint. A train moves in or out of the port four times a day, crossing under the New Jersey Turnpike and through a tangle of bridges and elevated freeways that carries 630,000 cars every day. Just across the turnpike, Newark Airport handles roughly 1,000 flights a day.

Testifying one month after the September attacks, Rear Admiral Richard Larrabee, the port commerce director, told a Senate Commerce, Science, and Transportation subcommittee, "As a port director, I cannot give you or my superiors a fair assessment today of the adequacy of current security procedures in place, because I am not provided with information on the risk analysis conducted to institute these measures."

If a container holding heroin slips into the United States, the street price may go down, gangs may be enriched, and drug use may rise. If that same container held chemical or biological agents, or a nuclear weapon, the social costs would be incalculable. Doing nothing to deter such events would be foolish, but doing everything possible would be more foolish still. "There are two things to be considered with regard to any scheme," Jean Jacques Rousseau once observed. "In the first place, 'Is it good in itself?' In the second, 'Can it be easily put into practice?'" In the case of homeland security the answers are yes, and absolutely not.

Some measures, both quotidian and provident, will be taken. Practical approaches to making air travel safe again will emerge incrementally. Newly integrated databases will prevent a recurrence of the dark comedy of errors that allowed many of the hijackers into the country in the first place. Postal workers, it is to be hoped, will be tested for the presence of biological agents with the same alacrity that senators are. But the culture itself will not be re-engineered. America will continue to be a place of tremendous economic dynamism and openness.

At the port the country's muscular determination to remain in business is manifest on every loading dock. But if one looks hard enough, the cost of openness is there to see. In a quiet spot amid the industrial bustle—behind Metro Metals, on the north side of the port facility—is a nasty clump of twisted metal. Some of the girders from the World Trade Center, another brawny symbol of U.S. economic strength that also happens to be owned by the Port Authority, have come to rest here. The stink of that day—the burnt smell of implacable mayhem—hangs near, reminding us that great symbols make irresistible targets.

Foreign Policy Reconsidered

Michael Ignatieff

Is the Human Rights Era Ending?

Since the end of the cold war, human rights has become the dominant moral vocabulary in foreign affairs. The question after Sept. 11 is whether the era of human rights has come and gone.

If that sounds alarmist, consider some of the evidence. Western pressure on China to honor human rights, never especially effective, has stopped altogether. Chinese support for the war on terror has secured Western silence about repression in the Xinjiang region. China now says it has a problem there with Islamic fundamentalists and terrorists, and it is straining to link them to Al Qaeda.

Michael Ignatieff is professor of human rights policy at the Kennedy School of Government at Harvard.

Meanwhile, Chancellor Gerhard Schröder of Germany, presented with evidence of Qaeda involvement in Chechnya, calls for a "differentiated evaluation" of Russian policy there. This new evaluation seems certain to involve forgetting that Moscow's war against terror has actually been waged against a whole people, costing tens of thousands of lives.

A similar chill is settling over world politics. Australia's government uses the threat of terrorism to justify incarcerating Afghan refugees in a desert compound. Tajikistan and Uzbekistan have leveraged their provision of bases and intelligence into a carte blanche for domestic repression. Egypt, which for many years has used detention without trial, military courts and torture to keep control of militants, now demands an even freer hand. Sudan, which was under attack from a coalition of liberals and black churches determined to end slavery and stop Khartoum's war against the south, is now accepted as an ally against Osama bin Laden. And President Robert Mugabe of Zimbabwe has decided that his longtime political opponents are really "terrorists."

Human Rights Watch has condemned these developments as opportunism, but something more durable than that may be at work. Rome has been attacked, and Rome is fighting to re-establish its security and its hegemony. This may permanently demote human rights in the hierarchy of America's foreign policy priorities.

Of course, just because the United States has other priorities doesn't have to mean that, in global terms, the era of this movement is over. Human rights has gone global by going local, anchoring itself in struggles for justice that can survive without American inspiration or leadership. The movement does not have its headquarters in Washington. But if Washington turns away, the movement loses the one government whose power can be decisive in stopping human rights abuses.

Activists may not see it this way, but their influence may have peaked in the 1990's. That was the decade when new constitutions brought human rights principles to the states created in the Soviet breakup, when United Nations agencies finally got the courage to tackle violations by member states, when America's State Department actively promoted human rights and democracy abroad. This was the era of humanitarian intervention in Bosnia, Kosovo and East Timor, the heyday of the United Nations tribunals in The Hague and Arusha, Tanzania.

In the humanitarian interventions of the 1990's, political figures like Prime Minister Tony Blair of Britain believed that they were ushering in a new era, backing human rights principles with political will and military steel. In reality, it was only an interregnum, made possible because Western militaries had spare capacity and time to do human rights work. Now with America launched on an indefinite military campaign against terrorists, will there be the political energy necessary to mount humanitarian interventions? The intellectual and political climate of a war on terror now resembles the atmosphere of the cold war. Then the imperative of countering Soviet and Chinese imperial advances trumped concern for the abuses of authoritarian governments in the Western camp. The new element in determining American foreign policy is what assets—bases, intelligence and diplomatic leverage—it can bring to bear against Al Qaeda.

Some veterans of the human rights campaigns of the cold war refuse to admit that the climate is any worse now than it was then. But in the Reagan years, the movement merely risked being unpopular. In the Bush era, it risks irrelevance.

Divided between horror at the attacks and alarm at being enlisted as moral cheerleaders in a war on terror, many European human rights groups are sitting on the sidelines. American groups like Human Rights Watch have turned themselves into war reporters, subjecting American military conduct to tough scrutiny on issues ranging from prisoner detention to collateral damage. Still others have teamed up with civil libertarians to defend rights and freedoms at home.

But the movement will have to engage soon in the battle of ideas: it has to challenge directly the claim that national security trumps human rights. The argument to make is that human rights is the best guarantor of national security. The United States, to encourage the building of secure states that do not harbor or export terror, will have to do more than secure base agreements. It will have to pressure these countries to provide basic political rights and due process. As the cold war should have taught us, cozying up to friendly authoritarians is a poor bet in the long term. America is still paying a price for its backing of the shah of Iran. In the Arab world today, the United States looks as if it is on the side of Louis XVI in 1789; come the revolution in Egypt or Saudi Arabia, American influence may be swept away.

The human rights movement is not in the business of preserving American power. But it should be concerned about stability, about moving strategically vital states like Egypt and Saudi Arabia from closed to open societies without delivering them up to religious fundamentalists. Nobody's rights in Egypt will be furthered if the state collapses into anarchy or fundamentalist absolutism. If the movement hopes to have a future, it has to advocate its objectives—freedom, participation, due process—in a way that addresses the necessity to create political stability. This doesn't mean suddenly going silent about arbitrary arrests and military courts. It means moving from denunciation alone to engagement, working with local activists, and with the parts of the government that will listen, moving these societies back from the precipice.

The movement aims at defending the rights of ordinary people. To do this, it has to help them construct strong civil societies and viable states. If it can't find new ways of achieving that goal, it will be remembered as a fashionable cause of the dim and distant 1990's.

Ivo H. Daalder and James M. Lindsay

Security Comes with Building Peace, Not Just Barriers

In his State of the Union speech last week, President Bush declared that "whatever it costs to defend our country, we will pay it." The budget he will unveil tomorrow makes good on that pledge. It will propose the largest real increase in defense spending since the Korean War and would double spending on homeland defense.

But the president's speech made no mention of foreign assistance for any place other than Afghanistan, no allusion to exploring a modern-day Marshall Plan focused on depriving extremist leaders of the desperate people willing to kill themselves and others.

This omission could prove to be the Achilles' heel of America's campaign against terrorism. More bombs abroad and better barriers at home will make it more difficult for potential terrorists to do us harm. But it won't stop them from trying—and succeeding. As one Irish Republican Army member said after failing to kill British Prime Minister Margaret Thatcher: "Remember, we have only to be lucky once. You will have to be lucky always."

So the question that we as a nation ought to be asking—even if our leaders are not—is whether securing our safety requires doing more than just preparing for war and new acts of terrorism. Do we also need to address the anti-Americanism that permeates the Arab-Islamic world, an area of more than a billion people stretching from Morocco to Indonesia, from Kazakhstan to Nigeria? And, if we do, are we willing to spend at least some of our money on the types of costly programs that helped rebuild Europe and Japan after World War II and effectively converted our enemies into friends?

Like the eagle on the dollar bill, which clutches an olive branch in one talon and arrows in the other, we could strike a balance. We can afford to try to build peace at the same time we're building bombs.

Military might

Not everyone believes such a balance is necessary. Some note that most people who hate us will never hurt us. They believe, as syndicated columnist Charles Krauthammer does, that anger and resentment at the United States "is a constant. The variable factor is whether America commands respect or contempt." In other words, if we punish our enemies, no one will dare attack us or help those who would.

Krauthammer has a point. Al-Qaida is on the run because of our military might; it's not because, as he correctly if sarcastically writes, "the president hosted Muslim envoys for a White House Iftar dinner."

But it is the tyrant's fallacy to believe that intimidation alone can produce security. We can depose regimes that support terrorists, yet the vulnerability of our society enables small groups of people to inflict tremendous harm on us even without a government sponsor. Osama bin Laden was a guest of the Taliban in Kandahar, but Mohamed Atta plotted the hijackings in Hamburg and Miami.

Looked at that way, addressing anti-Americanism is essential to our security. Not because hatred of the United States turns people automatically into terrorists, but because it gives terrorists what they need most—people willing to support them. If terrorists are shunned by the people they claim to represent, they are far easier to defeat.

We can never eliminate anti-Americanism entirely. Its causes extend beyond poverty and oppression. Bin Laden and his ilk will always hate us because they reject our values. They see our tolerance, materialism and pluralism as decadent and hollow. And as long as we are a great power, we will inspire envy and resentment in some.

Fortunately, few people's hatred runs that deep. Most people in the Arab-Islamic world reject bin Laden's medieval worldview. They avidly consume Western culture—witness the popularity of McDonald's restaurants and Hollywood movies. They admire America's capitalist spirit and democratic values. A poll taken last fall found that more than 80 percent of the people living in the Arab-Islamic world saw America as a land of opportunity. Less than 20 percent dismissed our democratic appeal.

Still, many people in the Arab-Islamic world are also convinced that we are indifferent, if not hostile, to their plight. They've heard us describe ourselves as defenders of democracy but seen us embrace authoritarian governments. They've heard us trumpet our generosity but seen little evidence of it in their own lives. They've watched us bomb Afghanistan but seen us shy away from the difficult task of rebuilding war-torn countries. We should not be surprised when they ask: "Why should we feel pity for your travails when you seem so uninterested in ours?"

Diminishing anti-Americanism will be difficult. In some cases, we are dealing with deeply ingrained perceptions, not facts. Many in the Arab-Islamic world forget that we rescued Somalia from famine and intervened militarily to protect Muslims in Bosnia and Kosovo. Yet, misunderstandings run so deep that, even now, many in the Arab-Islamic world insist that bin Laden was not responsible for Sept. 11.

Better public diplomacy is a must. U.S. officials should appear regularly on news outlets such as Al-Jazeera to make America's case to the world. Washington should also step up efforts to broadcast its message to the region through Voice of America and increased cultural and educational exchanges. President Bush's call to double the number of Peace Corps volunteers will be a help as well. To know us may not be to love us, but it may mean hating us less.

Public diplomacy, though, can only do so much. We must ultimately match our words with deeds.

New Marshall Plan

The Bush administration has pledged $297 million over the next year for Afghanistan's reconstruction. But Washington needs to think in terms larger than Afghanistan.

We should apply the lessons learned after World War II. Then, we spent billions of dollars to rebuild Germany and Japan, giving our former enemies a stake in creating productive and democratic societies. We could do the same today by working with our allies to develop a new Marshall Plan to address the hopelessness that poverty breeds and terrorists thrive on. People who have hope for a better future — a steady job and better means to provide for their families—will be less likely to blame America and others for their ills.

The Bush administration appears to have weighed in on this issue already. The New York Times reported last week that diplomats said the administration had rejected a (British-led) effort to persuade wealthy nations to increase their total foreign aid by $50 billion annually, double what they currently give. The administration has said that before increasing aid, donors should ensure they pick more effective projects and the countries getting the money should reduce corruption.

One major problem in motivating other Americans to fund a new Marshall plan is that many think we already spend a lot on foreign aid. A 1995 University of Maryland poll found that on average Americans believe that we spend 15 percent of the federal budget on foreign aid. This year, a 15 percent contribution would equal nearly $300 billion. If that were true, we would already have a new Marshall Plan.

But we actually spend only a half a penny out of every federal dollar on foreign aid, or about $12 billion annually. This is only one-fourth of President Bush's proposed $48 billion increase in defense spending. It is also puny by our historical standards. The Marshall Plan consumed 1.5 percent of our gross domestic product, a number 15 times higher than today. And we launched the Marshall Plan at a time when we also were dramatically increasing defense spending to combat the Soviet threat.

Foreign aid is no magic bullet. If it were, Egypt, which has received more than $55 billion in aid from the West over the past 25 years, would be prosperous today. But spent wisely, such aid can make a difference. It can help friendly states develop the law enforcement capabilities they need to track and capture terrorists in their midst. It can improve people's health and living conditions. It can be used to teach farmers to become more productive, so that fewer people will starve. It can also give people a stake in the global economy and can create common interests with us and a reason to work together.

More foreign aid can also be used to counter institutions in the Arab-Islamic world that preach anti-Americanism, including schools. America is better off if Pakistani and Palestinian children go to publicly funded schools that teach them a broad curriculum rather than to privately funded religious schools that teach hatred of America and intolerance of others. But that takes additional resources, so that there are enough public schools to give all the kids at least a basic education.

Aid could also be used to bolster the emergence of civil societies. One key way to do that is to financially support the networks of local groups that are independent of government control and central to democratization. Human rights monitors can hold governments accountable. Trade unions can protect the rights of laborers. Development organizations can provide training and credits to help women set up small businesses. And political groups can nurture viable oppositions.

A new Marshall Plan will not eliminate anti-Americanism. That goal is as unachievable as ridding the world of evil. What these policies can do is lower the flames of anti-Americanism. And that would contribute as much as bombs and barriers to bolstering our security.

Credits

Binder, Sarah and Bill Frenzel. "The Business of Congress after September 11." *Brookings Policy Dialogue*, no. 1, (February 2002): 1-8. Copyright © The Brookings Institution. Reprinted by permission of The Brookings Institution.

Carr, David. "The Futility of 'Homeland Defense.'" *Atlantic Monthly* (January 2002): 53-55. Copyright © 2002 David Carr. Reprinted with permission.

Cohen, Adam. "Keeping an Eye on Things." *On Magazine* (December 2001): 49-54. Copyright © 2001 Time Inc. reprinted by permission.

Daalder, Ivo H. and James M. Lindsay, "Security Comes with Building Peace, Not Just Barriers." *San Jose Mercury News* (February 3, 2002). Copyright © 2002 San Jose Mercury News. All rights reserved. Reproduced with permission.

Dorf, Michael C. "The Supreme Court Returns, To a Changed Legal Landscape." retrieved Wednesday, October 3, 2001 from www.findlaw.com/dorf/20011003.html. Reprinted by permission of the author. Copyright © 2001 Michael C. Dorf.

Fletcher, George P. "War and the Constitution." *The American Prospect*, vol. 13, no. 1 (January 1-14, 2002). Reprinted with permission from The American Prospect, 5 Broad Street, Boston, MA 02109. All rights reserved.

Freedberg, Sydney J., Jr. and Marilyn Werber Serafini,"Health and Welfare: Contagious Confusion." *National Journal* (November 9, 2001). Reprinted with permission. Copyright © 2001 National Journal Group, Inc.

Ignatieff, Michael. "Is the Human Rights Era Ending?" *New York Times* (February 5, 2002). Copyright © 2002 The New York Times. Reprinted with permission.

Katz, Lewis R. "Anti-Terrorism Laws: Too Much of a Good Thing." Case Western Reserve University School of Law. Originally published by *Jurist: The Legal Education Network* (jurist.law.pitt.edu). Reprinted by permission of the author.

Ornstein, Norman. "Mail Drop: Can Congress Recover from 9/11?" *The New Republic* (January 14, 2002): 10-12. Reprinted by permission of The New Republic, Copyright © 2002, The New Republic, LLC.

Posner, Richard A. "Security Versus Civil Liberties." *Atlantic Monthly* (December 2001): 46-4. Copyright © 2001 Richard A. Posner. Reprinted with permission.

Rahn, Richard W. "The Case Against Federalizing Airport Security." retrieved from www.cato.org/people/rahn.html. Reprinted with permission. Copyright © 2001 Cato Institute.

Rosenbaum, David E. "Since Sept. 11, Lobbyists Use New Pitches for Old Pleas." *New York Times* (December 3, 2001). Copyright © 2001 The New York Times. Reprinted with permission

Samuelson, Robert J. "Unwitting Accomplices?" *Washington Post* (November 7, 2001): A29. Copyright © 2001, The Washington Post Writers Group. Reprinted with permission.

Singer, P.W. "Arguments Against Federalization Flimsy." *Baltimore Sun* (November 7, 2001). Copyright © 2001 The Baltimore Sun. Reprinted with permission.

Taylor, Stuart Jr. "The Media, the Military, and Striking the Right Balance." *National Journal* (Oct. 22, 2001). Reprinted with permission. Copyright © 2001 National Journal Group, Inc.

Telhami, Shibley. "Arab and Muslim America: A Snapshot." *Brookings Review* , vol. 20, no. 1 (winter 2002): 1-15. Reprinted with permission. Copyright © 2002 The Brookings Institution.

Wallison, Peter J. "In Favor of Military Tribunals." *Christian Science Monitor* (January 3, 2002). Reprinted by permission of the author. Copyright © 2002 Peter J. Wallison.

"What September 11 Really Wrought." *The Economist* (January 12, 2002): 23-25. Copyright © 2002 The Economist Newspaper Group, Inc. Reprinted with permission. Further reproduction prohibited. www.economist.com

Yeoman, Barry and Bill Hogan. "Airline Insecurity." *Mother Jones* (January/February 2002): 41-47. Copyright © 2002, Foundation for National Progress. Reprinted with permission.